D1449713

Copyright © 2000 by Scholastic Inc.

———•———

All rights reserved. Published by Scholastic Inc.
DEAR AMERICA®, SCHOLASTIC, and associated logos are trademarks and/or registered trademarks of Scholastic Inc.

ISBN 0-439-24998-8

10 9 8 7 6 5 4 3 2 1   0/0 01 02 03 04 05

The display type was set in Capone, Caslon Antique,
Nicholas Cochin, and Herculanum.
The text type was set in Bembo.
Book design by Elizabeth B. Parisi

Printed in the U.S.A.
First printing, September 2000

———•———

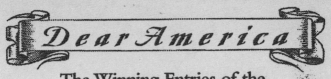

Dear America

The Winning Entries of the
Third Annual Student Writing Contest

PIKADON-DON
The World War II Diary of Rieko Murasako
Nagasaki, Japan, 1945

By Jodie Hillyard

THE JOURNEY TO A NEW LAND
The Diary of Hattie Simalina Potch
Mayflower, 1620

By Sara Doran

THE DIARY OF EDWARD DANIEL PHILLIPS
A Union Soldier
Pennsylvania, 1863

By Nathan Sadasivan

VOLCANO OF MONT PELÉE
THE DIARY OF NICOLE MAILHOT
SAINT-PIERRE, MARTINIQUE, CARIBBEAN, 1902
BY NICOLE HILLYARD

Scholastic Inc. New York

A Letter From the Publisher of Dear America

Dear Readers:

I'm proud to present the award-winning entries in Scholastic's Arrow Book Club Dear America Writing Contest. Scholastic received nearly 6,000 entries from students around the country from November 1999 through Winter 2000.

In this book you will find an introduction by noted educator Dick Abrahamson, who has provided teachers a way to use this book in classrooms. Additionally, there is the letter author Barry Denenberg wrote to the winners of the contest. And, of course, there are the winning entries themselves, which represent a range of personal experience and historical events — all beautifully written. We've also included biographical information about the authors.

The Dear America series is entering its fifth year of publication. The series' success is based on the brilliant work our authors do in every book that they write for Dear America. And the reason for this contest is to create new authors for the future.

I want to thank Scholastic Book Clubs for making this contest possible — and readers like you for being fans of Dear America.

Sincerely,

— *Jean Feiwel*
Publisher & Senior Vice President

Introduction

———•———

Written by Richard F. Abrahamson, Ph.D., Professor of Literature for Children and Young Adults, University of Houston, Houston, Texas.

For the past three years I have had the privilege of judging the Dear America Student Writing Contest. I have been inspired by the thousands of entries I have read and, of course, by the extraordinary proficiency of the winners. Congratulations to all!
Sincerely,
Barry Denenberg

Teachers know about carrying stacks of student papers home to be read and evaluated in our "spare time." It is part of the job. But how about 6,000 compositions?

Each year, Scholastic's Dear America Student Writing Contest continues to gain popularity with teachers and their students across the country. Again, this year, youngsters were asked to create diary entries showing the life of a fictional or real character (similar to the Dear America heroes) within a particular time in history. The events, places, and characters had to be historically accurate.

Thousands of students accepted the challenge, and what awaits you in this book are the award-winning student entries. These engaging stories can serve as models for student writing in elementary and middle school classrooms. The winning entries also serve as models in another way. As you read the students' comments about their writing and their lives, you'll read a testament to the power of parents engaged in their child's education, and the importance that a word of encouragement from a teacher can have on a youngster. You'll also read about how an eleven-year-old overcame writer's block; how a nine-year-old learned the value of doing extra research "just to make sure my story was historically accurate"; and how one writer took almost as much time revising his winning entry as it took to write the entire first draft. In all of the stories you'll see the winning combination of writing talent, diligence, and discipline. From six weeks to three months, these writers researched, wrote, revised, and enjoyed themselves. Grand-prize author Jodie Hillyard says it this way: "During the three months it took to write this book, I referred back to many of the Dear America diaries for ideas. My advice for anyone who sets a goal for himself or herself is to work hard, put your heart into whatever you do, and have fun doing it."

Jodie's story is set in Nagasaki, Japan, in 1945. *Pikadon-don: The World War II Diary of Rieko Murasako* serves as a fine example of how careful research on Japanese customs and events can be interwoven into a gripping tale about life just before and after the atom bomb was dropped. Rieko's beautiful descriptions of the gardens in Nagasaki are juxtaposed with matter-of-fact entries about the war. "Today was a quiet and fun day. We had no bomb raids today."

Against the backdrop of war, Rieko learns the wisdom of Japanese proverbs that will sustain her during the horrors to come. "If you carry a cedar cane it will help you reach your goals . . ."

"The cypress tree symbolizes hope. Its Japanese name means 'tomorrow it will happen.'"

As the diary continues, readers learn about the Potsdam Declaration and the atomic bombs dropped on Hiroshima and Nagasaki. Reiko's diary entries describing the effects of the bomb in Nagasaki are a model for painting pictures with words. "A lot of them had skin blackened by burns. They had no hair because their hair was burned. At a glance he couldn't tell whether he was looking at them from in front or in back. Their skin seemed to hang from their bodies." Later, Rieko writes, "The people that were in the city or close to it called it a *pika* (flash) because they never heard the sound of the explosion. Those outside the city who heard the *don* (boom) are calling it *pikadon* (flash-boom) or *pikadon-don* (flash-boom-boom). They use the nickname as a way to deal with what has happened."

Just as Jodie Hillyard used the other Dear America books for ideas, teachers will want to use her story as an example of student writing that shows how historical research can be integrated into an exciting tale; how simple description can paint vivid pictures; and how the human spirit can triumph even in the face of tragedy. Contrast and compare Rieko's adventure with these award-winning picture books: *Hiroshima No Pika* by Toshi Maruki; *Sadako*, written by Eleanor Coerr and illustrated by Ed Young; and *Faithful Elephants: A True Story of Animals, People and War*, written by Yukio Tsuchiya and illustrated by Ted Lewin for a fruitful thematic unit on World War II. Rieko's diary also works as a solid introduction to other Dear America and My Name Is America titles about the war: *My Secret War: The World War II Diary of Madeline Beck* by Mary Pope Osborne; *One Eye Laughing, the Other Weeping: The Diary of Julie Weiss* by Barry Denenberg; *The Journal of Scott Pendleton Collins: A World War II Soldier* by Walter Dean Myers; and *The Journal of Ben Uchida: Citizen 13559, Mirror Lake Internment Camp* by Barry Denenberg.

From World War II and Japan, move back in time to America in 1620. Eleven-year-old Sara Doran's prize-winning entry is *The Journey to a New Land: The Diary of Hattie Simalina Potch, Mayflower, 1620*. Hattie's diary brings readers into the cramped quarters of the *Mayflower*, where there is

"Just the smell of blood, spew, phlegm, and dirty diapers — not ever one whiff of fresh air."

This is a story of dreams: her parents' dream of a prosperous life in the New World and Hattie's very different dream. Readers are hooked when Hattie's second diary entry reveals her dream and foreshadows the action to come. "I am a Puritan, have blond hair, black eyes, and light skin. I am very skinny, my hair is not curly but stringy, and I am ugly. If I tell you something, you have to promise to never tell. I wish more than anything that . . . that I was Dutch! I know that that is against all Puritan rules, but I don't care; the thing that I hate most is that I am a Puritan and I promise you that I have a tremendously exhilarating plan on how to become Dutch!"

Hattie's adventure has shades of a Charles Dickens tale with an orphanage, mistaken identities, adoptions, and new lives. It also introduces youngsters to the hardships and experiences of the early settlers in Plimouth.

Lovers of Dear America books will recognize the name of Hattie's friend, Remember, the main character in Kathryn Lasky's highly praised

Dear America book *A Journey to the New World: The Diary of Remember Patience Whipple.* Teachers will find rich connections between this student-written diary and Lasky's novel. Watching the video made from the Lasky book will add an important media component to this unit (see ordering information for the videos below). Students can also go behind the scenes of the movie production by heading for the following Internet site: http://scholastic.com/dearamerica/tv/memdiary.htm while teachers will find a Discussion Guide with student activities and an interview with Lasky at this web site: http://scholastic.com/dearamerica/books/guides/journey. htm.

Parents and a librarian played important roles in eleven-year-old Nathan Sadasivan's successful contest entry. *The Diary of Edward Daniel Phillips: A Union Soldier, Pennsylvania, 1863* came about when he heard about the Dear America writing contest at a library program. His subject was inspired by a family trip. "Near the beginning of third grade, we set off on a vacation around the eastern half of America. . . . We visited several Civil War sites, including Fort Sumter, where the war began, and Appomattox, where the war ended. Although I was a little reluctant to go to any of them, I came back from the trip a Civil War buff."

At the age of fifteen, Edward Daniel Phillips lies about his age and, filled with "patriotic fever," joins the Michigan Regiment as a Union soldier. Edward uses his journal to record the killing, courage, confusion, and camaraderie he witnesses in the Civil War battle at Gettysburg. His gripping description of being in the fight at Cemetary Ridge serves to illustrate the quality of the writing in this narrative. "A few moments later, more Rebels appeared. They fired one more volley at us, then surged forward. In a few moments we were face to face with what seemed like twenty thousand Rebs. With rifle barrels literally touching, both sides would let volley after volley fly into enemy lines. It was almost impossible for a bullet not to find its mark, but at times a rifle barrel could get so hot that it would explode and kill its own master. It was the goriest, bloodiest fight that I have ever seen. One Reb put a red handkerchief around his head.

The color made an inviting target, and almost immediately a bullet cracked open his skull."

Nathan Sadasivan does an especially good job of blending real people with fictional characters. A note at the end of the diary points out to readers the real people mentioned throughout the story from Robert E. Lee to Ulysses S. Grant to John Reynolds and General Weed. *The Diary of Edward Daniel Phillips: A Union Soldier* will work nicely as an introduction to a unit on the Civil War featuring the following books from the Dear America and My Name Is America series: *The Journal of James Edmond Pease: A Civil War Union Soldier* by Jim Murphy; *When Will This Cruel War Be Over? The Civil War Diary of Emma Simpson* by Barry Denenberg; *A Light in the Storm: The Civil War Diary of Amelia Martin* by Karen Hesse; *I Thought My Soul Would Rise and Fly: The Diary of Patsy, a Freed Girl* by Joyce Hansen; and *A Picture of Freedom: The Diary of Clotee, A Slave Girl* by Patricia McKissack.

The final award winner in this collection comes from nine-year-old Nicole Hillyard. If the last name sounds familiar, she is the sister of grand-prize winner Jodie Hillyard. Nicole's survival story, *Volcano of Mont Pelée: The Diary of Nicole Mailhot, Saint-Pierre, Martinique, Caribbean*, takes place in 1902. Nicole Mailhot loves her hometown of Saint-Pierre and is not at all pleased that her ship-building father is crafting a boat to take them to America — to Rhode Island and opportunity.

The volcano that looms over Saint-Pierre provides the tension in this piece of exciting writing. Nicole's father works harder on the boat as the volcano becomes active once again. "On the twenty-fifth the volcano started to spit ash and gas. It has been covering every thing and everybody with gray dust. People are having a hard time breathing because of the gases. My throat has been sore and my eyes feel like they are burning all the time. Père says that a lot of animals in Saint-Pierre have been dying because of the poisonous gases. They suffocated. Sometimes I feel like I'm suffocating too."

As the family frantically readies to leave the island, government troops stop the residents from departing. Nicole and her family sneak past the guards at night and hide in the boat waiting for their detained father to return. Beaten but alive, he arrives at the boat and they cast off. They look back at their homeland only to watch the volcano erupting.

Some days later, from the safety of her boat moored in Rhode Island, Nicole describes the tragedy they narrowly missed. "The paper said that the boulders that we saw shoot from the crater were travelling about three hundred miles per hour. The red glowing cloud made a hurricane force and leveled everything in its path. The surge of steam was believed to be about 1,800 degrees Fahrenheit. It melted glass, twisted the heaviest steel beams and turned wood into charcoal instantly. Everyone who tried to breathe the air died immediately. The heat completely shriveled their lungs." In all, 34,000 people lost their lives in three minutes' time.

Volcano of Mont Pelée is about courage and the importance of a strong family and, as such, dovetails beautifully with these Dear America titles: *Across the Wide and Lonesome Prairie: The Oregon Trail Diary of Hattie Campbell* by Kristiana Gregory; *The Great Railroad Race: The Diary of Libby West* by Kristiana Gregory; *Dreams in the Golden Country: The Diary of Zipporah Feldman, a Jewish Immigrant Girl* by Kathryn Lasky; and two books in the new My America series for younger readers, *Our Strange New Land: Elizabeth's Diary, Jamestown, Virginia, 1609* by Patricia Hermes and *My Brother's Keeper: Virginia's Diary, Gettysburg, Pennsylvania, 1863* by Mary Pope Osborne.

So, welcome to this collection of winning stories from the latest Dear America writing contest. May they serve as creative-writing models for your students and as introductions to thematic units that include other titles in the Dear America series. May these talented students also remind you of the positive, powerful impact created when parents and teachers work together to provide the best education for all children. To that end, let me give eleven-year-old Sara Doran the final word.

"I love to write! In the second and third grades I had a teacher, Ms. Forsstrom, who encouraged me to write and enter contests. In the third grade I entered a writing contest for the local newpaper. The story had to be a mystery and at least one paragraph long. I wrote about two pages and won! It was the first time my writing had ever been published and I was very excited. I believe that I owe all my writing success to my very supportive family and to Ms. Forsstrom. I would like to thank them all for everything."

Sources for Dear America Teaching Materials

The videos made from the Dear America books are available from Scholastic for $12.95 plus shipping and handling by calling toll-free 1-877-750-7111.

Teachers can find a Discussion Guide for each of the Dear America, My Name Is America, My America, and Royal Diaries on the web at: http://scholastic.com/dearamerica/books/guides /index.htm. These guides include questions about each novel, student activities, and an interview with each of the authors.

Look for more information on the next Dear America Writing Contest by visiting http:// scholastic.com/dearamerica/index.htm.

A Letter to the Winning Writers from Dear America Author and Contest Judge, Barry Denenberg

Dear DEAR AMERICA CONTEST winners:

I offered to judge SCHOLASTIC'S DEAR AMERICA WRITING CONTEST because I believe that the DEAR AMERICA books are a compelling way to "teach" American history. The many letters I have received confirm my belief.

The response to the contest was gratifying — nearly six thousand entries were received. Some were "aged" with teas, some tied with ribbons and illustrated, and others neatly printed on word processors. There were entire classes that participated.

The overwhelming majority of entries were sincere, thoughtful, and the result of hard work.

But contests demand winners and each entry was read and judged on:

> *— storytelling ability*
> *— grasp of history*
> *— command of the language*
> *— characterization*
> *— emotional content*

Your diary was not only well written, nicely crafted, accurate, and intelligent but you cared about what you were writing.

Your entry had heart.

This is what made it superlative.

It was a privilege to judge this contest, and my reward was seeing the wonder of your imagination and feeling the power of your prose each time I read your diary.

Please convey my appreciation to your family and teachers, who I am sure played an important part.

Keep up the good work.

—Barry Denenberg.

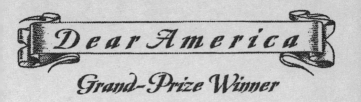

Dear America

Grand-Prize Winner

PIKADON-DON

The World War II Diary of Rieko Murasako Nagasaki, Japan, 1945

BY JODIE HILLYARD

Nagasaki, Japan
1945

August 1, 1945

Dear Diary,

There is so much I want to tell you today.

As I woke up this *gozaimasu* (morning,) I went to the windowsill. I stretched out my arms and took a deep breath of the cool, crisp morning air. The birds were singing in the sweet-smelling cherry trees, outside my window. The tiny crickets were chirping beneath my windowsill. What a beautiful day it was today. It's lovely here. There are so many beautifully designed buildings here in Nagasaki. Here in the hills outside the city, there are tall trees with many different varieties of flowers. I love the way the long bridges run across the water. This is my favorite place in the whole world. When I look at this beauty, it's hard to believe a war is going on now. A war that is being called World War II. I could have stood by my window all day long today, daydreaming about its beauty if it weren't for my older *ane* (sister) Yasuko. She is seventeen years old. She ran in and told me I'm late for *asa-gohan* (breakfast) and must hurry. Chichi (Father) won't be happy.

When I sat down for *asa-gohan*, Chichi gave me a stern look. My grandparents and my family were all staring at me. Everyone was very quiet. Then Chichi said, "Enjoy your meal." I was so relieved he didn't punish me. We had my favorite, miso soup. I like the way the fish, seaweed, tofu, and soybean curd taste when mixed with soybean-and-grain broth. After I had sipped the broth, I began eating the rest with my *hashi* (chopsticks.) Then I looked over at my little brother, Eiji, and began to giggle. He was stabbing the fish with one of his *hashi*. He didn't think anyone would notice. Maybe that's because he is only *san* (three) years old. Just as he was about to stick the piece of fish in his mouth, Haha (Mother) caught sight of him. After scolding him, Chichi scolded me for giggling. He said that I was only encouraging him to do the wrong thing by laughing. Because everyone knows *hashi* must not be licked, waved in the air, left in a rice dish, or used to stab the food. He punished me and told me that I had to do all the dishes by myself today. For a family of eight, that was a lot of dishes.

After I washed the dishes, I practiced on the koto with Yasuko. This zitherlike instrument with thirteen strings lies flat on the floor in the corner of our living room. Yasuko is helping me learn it because I am not very good at it yet. She says I must practice more. My sobo (grandmother) tells me that I am doing fine. Although, I think she is just being kind. My older brother, Masahiro, he's eighteen years old, had to practice the shakuhachi. It sounds so pretty when he plays the music from this long bamboo flute. It makes me think of leaves dancing in the wind. I wish I had his talent.

Today we received a letter from my aunt Oba. I was excited to hear that they were all doing well but I don't like to hear from her too often. You see, my aunt Oba, my uncle Nijo, and my cousin Keiko left Japan for America seven years ago. Ever since then, they have been trying to get our family to move there. They say that the land is beautiful and provides many things. My father and mother always say, "Maybe someday but not today, because our lands are at war and it wouldn't be safe to go right now." I'm so relieved every time they say that. I could never imagine leaving Nagasaki to go to the other side of the world. I would miss my home and my surroundings but most of all my friends. I would especially miss my best friend, Masako Hachiya.

Masako and I do everything together. She is thirteen years old just like me. I like going over to her house. Masako's family rented a pet this week. She invited me over to play with it and stay for *ban-gohan* (dinner). My haha made me take Eiji, too. Masako and I weren't able to ride bikes today because Eiji is too young. Therefore, we played with Masako's rented pet, an armadillo, instead. We had a lot of fun seeing Eiji's reaction to it. After we played with the armadillo, Masako's mother called us in for dinner. Her mother made *unage* (eel), *sashimi* (raw fish), *oden* (fish cake stew), tofu, and *makizushi* (sushi roll) wrapped with *nori* (seaweed). She also made raw salmon and abalone, served on molded vinegar-flavored rice patties. We dipped them in some *shoyu* (soy sauce) and put a pinch of *wasabi* (horseradish paste) on them. Eiji did not like the food Mrs. Hachiya made, therefore he didn't eat much. I felt he was insulting Mrs. Hachiya's cooking and that embarrassed me. After dinner, as all Japanese families do, we had a cup of *cha* (green tea). I don't care for it that much. But Haha always said green tea is a miraculous medicine for the maintenance of health. It has the power to prolong life, prevent cavities, and fight viruses.

Masako is so lucky to be able to rent pets. Once, Eiji asked if we could rent a pet. Haha gave us a queer look and said she had too many animals running around the house as it is. I don't think she will ever let us rent one. After dinner, Sofu came to get us from the Hachiya's house.

Today was a quiet and fun day. We had no bomb raids today. I enjoyed today very much. Haha told us it was time for bed. I must go now. I will write you soon.

— Rieko

August 7, 1945

Dear Diary,

A lot has gone on in the last week. We have had many bomb raids while I was at school. The sirens are very loud and seem to pierce my ears. It seems like we didn't get much done at school this week because of all the bomb raids. Everytime we would get started on a project, the sirens would go off and we had to run to a shelter beneath the school. That seems like our daily routine until yesterday.

Yesterday was a terrible day. At around 8:30 A.M. the principal, Mr. Yokochi, made and announcement to the school. He said that at 8:15 A.M. a large explosion was set off in Hiroshima. Many people were hurt and killed. Therefore, they were closing the school for the day. That seemed odd to Masako and me. Up until now, many bombs had been dropped in different parts of Japan, but we have never been sent home from school before. This bomb must have been a bad one.

When I got home, I noticed that Masahiro

and Chichi were home from work. My parents and grandparents and Masahiro were all talking in the kitchen. All went quiet when I came through the door. No one said a word. They just looked at me. Haha, Chichi, and Masahiro had sad and worried looks on their faces. Then the silence broke when Eiji started to count. *Ichi*, (1), *ni* (2), *san* (3), *shi* (4), *go* (5), *shichi* (7). I laughed and said *roku* (6). Then he continued, *hachi* (8), *ku* (9), *ju* (10). We all clapped, and Chichi said, "Very good, Eiji." Eiji smiled and ran out of the room. Chichi told me to go and watch after him. He said the adults needed to talk now.

When I went into the other room, I saw Eiji on a pillow looking at a book. I also decided to look at a book I had been reading. My mind wasn't on the book, because I could hear my parents talking in the other room. Before I knew it, Eiji was asleep and I found myself over near the opening of the door, listening to them talk.

Masahiro told Haha that this wasn't an ordinary bomb, such as the ones dropped in Japan before. It was an atomic bomb. The damage in

Hiroshima was devastating. Chichi and Masahiro worked for the local paper. Chichi said that some of the people from the paper were going over to Hiroshima to find out exactly what was going on and the extent of the damage. It had been difficult to obtain information, for the city was isolated, all ordinary lines of communication had been destroyed. They came home early to tell Haha that they were going to have to work some long hours for the next few days. Haha shook her head and said she understood. Haha quickly gathered some food for them and then they left.

I heard someone coming. I quickly moved away from the door and pretended to read again. It was Sofu (grandfather). I hesitated and then asked Sofu what an atomic bomb was. He said that I should not be listening to other people's conversations. I told him that I knew that but couldn't help overhearing them talk. He said I should try harder. I felt bad for listening. Sofu put his arm around my shoulder and then he said he understood because he was thirteen once, too. He began to tell me that he really didn't know exactly what an atomic bomb was. He only knew that it was a much bigger bomb than anything else that had ever been used before. A lot of damage was done with it. The thought of that scared me. I asked, what if it happens here? What will we do then? He told me not to worry; everything would be just fine here. I think he sensed that it scared me because he changed the subject quickly. Sofu told me that the plants in the garden needed watering. He said that this is where he was heading before we started to talk. He asked if I wanted to help him. I said yes. The thought of the garden was a more pleasant subject.

I think Sofu and I like the garden the most. We always seem to get lost in its beauty. Even though it isn't that big. Whenever we get depressed, we can come here and feel good about life. When I got out there, I took a deep breath of cool air. Sofu began to water the plants. I could hear the trees moving from the breeze. We have quite a variety in our yard. Sofu came over and began to look at the trees with me. "Beautiful," he said. He asked which ones I liked the best. "I like them all," I said. He then gave me a different view of the trees. This was a view that I had never thought of before. He told me that the trees are very useful to us if we believe. I asked what he meant by if we believe. He then began to tell me some old Japanese proverbs. He started to point to the cedar trees and said, "If you carry a cedar cane, it will help you reach your goals." Then he pointed to the chestnut tree and said, "If you eat with chestnut chopsticks for a year, it will make you a millionaire." "Unfortunately we don't have any," I said. He continued, "The cypress tree symbolizes hope. Its Japanese name means 'tomorrow it will happen.'" He then pointed to the plum tree and said, "If you bite on a young plum branch, it will cure a toothache." Next he pointed to the zelkova tree and said he thinks that I would like this one the best because if we burned the wood it would keep the mice away for two years. He knows how much I dislike mice. "So which is your favorite?" he said. I thought about it for a moment and told him, "I think it is the cypress tree. We all need to be hopeful for tomorrow." Sofu smiled, put his arm around me again, and said that was his favorite, too. I felt much better. Then we finished watering the garden.

Later that evening I told Eiji his favorite story. I think it is his favorite because we act it out with our hands and arms. It is an ancient Japanese legend of how Japan began. It is called "The Islands Born from the Sea." It goes like this: From their heavenly home, Izanagi and Izanami spied the speck we call Earth. (We make circles with our fingers and put them to our eyes.) To see what it was like, they descended the Floating Bridge to Heaven. (We stretch our arms up high.) Izanagi thrust his jeweled spear into the sea, drew it out, and gave it a shake. (We thrust one arm out and bring it back, then shake it.) A drop of brine fell away and became Onogoro, Japan's first island. After that, Izanagi and Izanami had many children. Each was an island of Japan. (We point our pointer fingers down and make them go up and down.) Eiji kept saying, "Again." So I must have told him that story thirty times last night.

Today, Chichi and Masahiro came home for a short time. I overheard them say the conditions in Hiroshima were much worse than they thought. They began to tell Sofu how bad. The word is that the governments of the United States, England, and China have been trying to put a stop to the war. They have made a declaration called the Potsdam Declaration for the Japanese government to sign and agree to. Apparently our government and the premier of Japan, Mr. Suzuki, rejected the Potsdam Declaration as being unworthy of public notice. It was rejected because the declaration made no mention of the future status of the emperor. Keeping the emperor is something very important to our country. These other governments said there are no alternatives. Sign or be annihilated. The premier of Japan didn't believe they would do it. That is when the president of the United States of America, Harry Truman, ordered that a bomb be dropped. They dropped an atomic bomb they named "Little Boy" over Hiroshima. Apparently the bomb exploded 1800 feet above the ground and caused such a massive explosion that it leveled the city. People just disappeared. Anyone unprotected to a distance of about a mile from the point directly below the explosion were killed instantly. Others within five square miles were seriously hurt. No one has ever seen a bomb that could do that. Chichi said that everyone there is in a daze.

Chichi said, "The premier of Japan still wouldn't sign the Potsdam Declaration. What will happen next?" Why do people war? I'll never know. I just don't understand why everyone can't just get along. It hurts me to think about all those innocent people in Hiroshima. I must say good night now.
— Rieko

August 14, 1945

Dear Diary,

So many terrible things have happened since I wrote last. It seems like a dream. I'm having trouble sleeping at night and believing what happened.

On August 8 the Russians declared war on Japan, too.

On the ninth, the unimaginable happened.

All was quiet in the morning. Yasuko went to work as a seamstress as usual. Chichi and Masahiro stayed home from work to sleep for a while. They had been working such long hours. I told my haha that my stomach was hurting that morning so Haha told me to stay home from school. I really was just scared to be away from the family if another bomb went off. I was afraid I would never see them again. I am glad I did. I played with Eiji to keep him quiet till Chichi and Masahiro woke. Sofu and Sobo were in the garden having tea. Haha was completing after-breakfast chores.

At about 10:50, the sirens began to go off. I took Eiji and held him tight. Then the sirens stopped. The sirens and the radio had just given the all-clear signal. All was quiet again. Eiji began to play, and I went into the kitchen to get him something to drink. Then all of a sudden, at 11:00 A.M., I saw a bright *pika* (flash) outside the house. It was almost blinding like the sun had fallen from the sky. Then I heard a loud *don* (boom) and then another. They were so loud they made the earth shake beneath my feet. The thunderous sound from the *dons* made my ears ring. I ran to the window and saw a cloud of smoke billowing up at a distance. It was in the shape of a large mushroom. I feared that another atomic bomb was dropped in the city. Eiji began to cry. I ran to him and held him tight, close to the floor. I thought we were all going to die. All was quiet again.

Chichi ran out of his room and made sure everyone was all right. Then he asked, "Where's Yasuko?" Haha told him she was at work at the edge of the city. Chichi told us that he was going to find her to make sure she was all right. He jumped on his bike and sped away fast.

On his way to the city, there were many people heading out. He had to get off his bike because of the people blocking the way. He saw many of them were naked and in a daze. A lot of them had skin blackened by burns. They had no hair because their hair was burned. At a glance he couldn't tell whether he was looking at them from in front or in back. Their skin seemed to hang from their bodies. If there had been only one or two such people, perhaps it would not have had such a strong impression. But wherever he walked, he saw these people. Many of them died along the road.

No one was panicking as he expected. Everyone was moving in slow motion. People were moaning. Some were incapacitated. The rest were fleeing from the destruction. Some headed toward the rivers where they thought their families might be. Others hoped to find authorities or medical personnel there. Still others just walked with the crowd with no clear destination in mind. Chichi noticed some were jumping into the rivers to escape the heat. Others' clothes were on fire and were jumping in to put the fire out. People were pushing others into the water by the pressure of crowds at the riverbanks. A lot had drowned. When he spoke to individuals on the road, they said that they had been hit by something they didn't understand.

Those who were able walked silently toward the suburbs in the distant hills. Their spirit was broken. When asked where they were going, they pointed away from the city and said, "This way." They were so broken and confused that they looked like robots. I can picture them in my mind as Chichi told us.

He finally reached Yasuko's place of employment or what was left of it. It was about three thousand meters from the center of the explosion. The building had partially collapsed. He found her under part of a wall that had fallen. Yasuko looked fine. She had minor burns and only a few scratches. She told Chichi that she felt strange. So he insisted she see a doctor. He desperately looked for a doctor or a hospital. When he came upon a temporary hospital outside, he found that all of the people in that area were crowded around. He tried to get help for Yasuko, but he didn't seem to have any success.

Chichi remembered there was a hospital nearby in the city. He headed there with Yasuko. Nothing looked the same. There were dead bodies everywhere and many alive but just lying around. As they got closer to the city, it looked more like an empty field. There was debris everywhere. There was practically no room for them to walk.

Yasuko was getting sick and said she couldn't

walk anymore. So Chichi and Yasuko went to a nearby building where injured people were lying inside. She needed to sit down. She wanted water but there wasn't any. They were together with dead people in the building. Only they were not really inside the building because the building itself had been destroyed. Chichi couldn't figure out why all these people were suffering, or what illness it was that had struck them down. He only knew that it must have something to do with the bomb. He said, "People seemed to inhale something from the air, which we could not see."

Chichi decided to try to take Yasuko home so we could take care of her. He helped her get up and began to leave the area. But they were cut off from escape. Fires were beginning to spread out, and there was nowhere to go. They found another half-standing building and decided to rest for a while until the fires died down. Yasuko fell asleep. She never woke up again. I never got to say good-bye.

Chichi brought her home and we buried her near the trees by the garden.

We were told that the Russians invaded Manchuria, taking it over right after the bombing.

On August 10, the members of the supreme war council had a meeting to discuss the end of the war. I could not believe it. After all that Japan has gone through, neither the nation's leaders nor the people were willing to stop the fighting, no matter how hopeless it seemed. The only way they would sign the declaration and stop the war was if the throne could be preserved. The members of the council offered their varying ideas to the emperor. The arguing continued until Emperor Hirohito, who ordinarily never joined the council in their debates, stood up. He said, "Ending the war is the only way to restore world peace and to relieve the nation from this terrible distress." He advised the council to accept the Potsdam Declaration's terms. Then the emperor departed. Premier Suzuki rose and spoke. "His Majesty's decision should be made the decision of this conference as well." The council then agreed.

Emperor Hirohito was allowed to remain,

although he was stripped of all governing powers. Across the country, everyone listened with mixed emotions as Emperor Hirohito announced by radio that he was not divine anymore. Some felt humiliated because outside governments forced so many changes on Japan, while others felt relieved the war was over.

Today, August 14, the war was declared over. Many parts of Japan were destroyed. Because of the massive number of people who died, authorities began to cremate the bodies. This was both for the prevention of disease and in accordance with the Japanese custom. The smell from the crematories fill the air.

I hadn't heard from Masako and her family since the bombing. I decided to go over to her house and talk to her. Their house was empty. I pray that they are all right, but no one knows for sure.

— Rieko

August 29, 1945

Dear Diary,

Mr. Hachiya visited us today. He wanted to see how we were doing. I asked how Masako was. He said she had been injured but was doing better. They were at a hospital on a nearby island. He came back to get some clothes and then he would be heading back there. I asked what had happened to her. He told us that Masako was working with a classmate on a project at school when the bomb hit. He had been looking for her for two days. He found her at a classmate's house. She had minor burns and scratches. But her face was so distorted and changed that he didn't recognize her until she spoke and even then it was hard. He brought her to a hospital at a nearby island to be treated. She was doing better, and the swelling was going down. But he said her spirit was broken. He said that she had been asking about me. I told him that I was all right but we were all mourning over the loss of Yasuko. He expressed his remorse. He didn't know.

I told him to wait a minute; I had something for Masako. I quickly ran to my room and grabbed my favorite doll. The one Masako liked best, too. Then I ran outside and grabbed a branch from the cypress tree. When I came back inside, I gave them to Mr. Hachiya. I told him the doll was for Masako while we were apart. This way we could be close while far away. I then told him that the branch represented hope. Hope for a better tomorrow. I gave him a hug and asked him to give it to Masako. He said he would and that he was sure these things would help her get better faster. Then he left.

It has been almost three weeks since the bombing, and Chichi was sick.

Haha thought it was from the stress of losing Yasuko. Then he started to get spots all over his body. His hair began to fall out. He began to vomit small clumps of blood many times. Finally, he began to bleed all over his mouth. At times his fever was very high. Haha didn't know what it was. Not even the doctors were sure. They thought it was an epidemic because they were seeing the same thing happen all over the area.

So Haha told the rest of the family not to touch Chichi. We had to disinfect all utensils and everything that he used. We were all afraid of it. After twelve days of agony and torture, he died. Chichi must have inhaled from the air in the city that same strange disease that killed so many. People are calling it the A-bomb disease.

We buried him next to Yasuko near the trees by the garden.

I don't wish to write anymore. It only makes me depressed to think of such horror.

— Rieko

September 30. 1947 (Two Years Later)

Dear Diary,

I finally found you. I thought you were lost forever. Someone put you in one of our old trunks in the attic. It must have been when we moved to America.

After the war, we received a letter from Aunt Oba. She wanted to make sure we were all right. When she found out about Chichi and Yasuko, she again invited us to come to America. This time, Haha and Sofu decided it would be best if we did. They also feared the A-bomb disease would wipe out the rest of the family. We quickly packed and made arrangements to live with Aunt Oba in America.

I am fifteen years old now. We have learned that the atomic bomb named "Little Boy," which landed on Hiroshima, killed more than 71,000 people. The atomic bomb that landed on Nagasaki was named "Fat Man," and it killed more than 40,000 people. It landed in the valley of the Urakami River, detonating between two Mitsubishi plants, ending their usefulness as producers of torpedoes. Had it landed nearer the designated aiming point, in a field nearby, the damage and casualties would have been much greater.

I heard from Masako last month and she is doing better. She said that she gets sick a lot since the bomb. She, too, has a little bit of the A-bomb disease. The doctor said that the bomb put great amounts of radiation in the air. That is why so many people got sick and died after the explosion. Just like Chichi and Yasuko. She said it has poisoned her blood a little, too. The doctors are saying it looks like it is leukemia, a type of cancer, but no one is sure. They have been running all kinds of tests. She told me she is tired of all the needles.

Mr. Hachiya said she could come and visit me next month. He thinks she needs a change of pace. He said it would do her good. I can't wait. She is bringing me a new baby cypress tree to plant at my new home. It will be just like old times.

Masako told me that the city is being built up again and everything is changing. Many people have given the bombing a nickname. The people that were in the city or close to it called it *pika* (flash) because they never heard the sound of the explosion. Those outside the city who heard the *don* (boom) are calling it *pikadon* (flash-boom) or *pikadon-don* (flash-boom-boom). They use the nickname as a way to deal with what has happened.

I will never forget the horror that happened that day or how it changed my life forever. I will carry deep in my heart all the unhealed wounds and remorseful memories of all those that died that day in Nagasaki. All because of an atomic bomb that went *pikadon-don*.

In memory of Chichi and Yasuko and all that died, I dedicate this poem to them:

> *In Hiroshima, August 6, 1945,*
> *an A-bomb named Little Boy fell from the sky.*
> *The city destroyed and over 71,000 ceased,*
> *all because the governments said they were seeking peace.*
>
> *The United States, England, and China said annihilation*
> *if you don't sign the Potsdam Declaration.*
> *Japan said, "There's no provision for the Emperor.*
> *We will not sign if that doesn't occur."*
>
> *Therefore, in Nagasaki on August 9,*
> *an A-bomb named Fat Man dropped with all its might.*
> *In the valley of the Urakami River it lands,*
> *this time killing over 40,000.*
>
> *Emperor Hirohito said, "End the War."*
> *His governing powers he had no more.*
> *He was forced to announce it on the radio.*
> *"Divine no more," people heard high and low.*
>
> *The A-bomb disease, caused by radiation,*
> *killed Yasuko, Chichi, and most of the nation.*

Others got leukemia like Masako.
People were sick and had to lay low.

The cypress tree will help people cope
because it reminds and stands for tomorrow's hope.
I will never forget the horror that day
and the reasons why I feel this way.

The war is now over and people are gone
*all because of **Pikadon-don.***

— *Rieko*

About the Author

Of writing *Pikadon-don: The World War II Diary of Rieko Murasako,* Jodie Hillyard says, "I came up with the idea of basing my story in Nagasaki, Japan, because I have a pen pal named Rieko who lives in Japan. I used her first name for the main character in my story, but the story is not about her at all. I have always been fascinated with Japanese culture and chose Nagasaki because while most people know about the bombing of Hiroshima, the bombing of Nagasaki is often forgotten.

"I did lots of research for this story so it would be historically and culturally accurate. I borrowed more than twenty-five books from the library and used many of the history and research books I have at home. Although my characters are fictional, all of the things that happened to them happened to real people during the bombing.

"I tried to find as much information as I could on Japanese culture, from their food to their legends, giving readers a real feel of what it was like to live there. I tried to help readers understand why Nagasaki was bombed and how it affected so many innocent lives.

"During the three months it took to write this book, I referred back to many of the Dear America diaries for ideas. My advice to everyone who sets a goal before himself or herself is to work hard, put your heart into whatever you do, and have fun doing it."

Jodie Hillyard is twelve years old and lives in Londonderry, New Hampshire. She is home-schooled, and her hobbies are drawing, dancing, writing, reading, singing, poetry, song writing, and playing the piano. First-prize winner Nicole Hillyard is Jodie's sister.

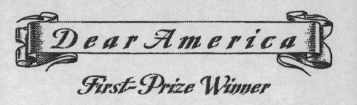

Dear America

First-Prize Winner

THE JOURNEY TO A NEW LAND

The Diary of Hattie Simalina Potch Mayflower, 1620

BY SARA DORAN

Mayflower,
1620

Dear Diary,

The harsh seas never stop. They thrash this ship that be called the *Mayflower*. Methinks that it was a big mistake going aboard a ship that will take thou to a new land with wild animals, no streets, no shops, and thou has heard that there are wild savages there that steal thou's hair! Thus many people are still journeying to this place were we shall stay forever. I must go now for I feel as if thou shall cast, and we have such little room, that it would reek for weeks!

Sincerely,

Hattie

October 6, 1620
Mayflower

Dear Diary,

I beg your pardon for not writing in a few days, but my brother Thomas cast all over the place and thou had to take care of him, and I even had to clean up his mess! This ship was much bigger when we boarded it than now with all these blasted people on it. I suppose you are wondering about me. Well I will tell you this, there is not much to know. I am a Puritan, have blond hair, black eyes, and light skin. I am very skinny, my hair is not curly but stringy, and I am ugly. If I tell you something, you have to promise to never tell. I wish more then anything that . . . that I was Dutch! I know that that is against all Puritan rules, but I don't care. The thing that I hate most is that I am a Puritan and I promise you that I have a tremendously exhilarating plan on how to become a Dutch!

Sincerely,

Hattie

October 9, 1620
Mayflower

Dear Diary,

My friend Tamilie Sinders and I just saw Lissy
Nickeson and Martha James walk on the ship in
their pink and blue dresses with their locks of
curls flowing down to their shoulders, with their
ruffles and flouncey dresses never swaying back
and forth. All the finest young men waiting at
their beck and call. Ohhhh! How envious I am
of them. They are so beautiful and thou is so
plain and ugly. By the way, Lissy and Martha are
Dutch!

Sincerely,
Plain and Envious Hattie

October 12, 1620
Mayflower

Dear Diary,

Today is a day of mourning for the Puritans.
You see thou's friend Sindra Saulington has gone

overboard. The wind was just too strong for the weak little thing. I have cried every night since 6:30 Monday October 9, the night of the accident. This is what supposedly happened that night. You see, Sindra was looking down onto the harsh and cold waters when suddenly a huge gust of wind came blowing and nearly turned the ship on its side. The whole crew ran down below not noticing that one small, pretty body was still left up there. Her cries and pleas were no match for the horrendous roar of the wind. The ship by now was nearly on its side with sounds of crying, screaming, prayers, and shouting, no one noticing that Sindra was up there. Well actually she wasn't up there. By that time her body had already taken that great plunge in the sea. The icy cruel sea of 5:30. Now no one except the captain and crew are allowed on the top of the *Mayflower* after 5:30.

Sincerely,
Hattie

October 15, 1602
Morning, *Mayflower*

Dear Diary,

Thou just remembered that you haven't met my parents! Well, I will introduce you to my mum first. Diary, this is my mum, Millie Rememberence Potch, and this is my father, Tam Potch. Aren't they sweet! My mum teaches me stuff that I will need to know so that when we reach this "New World" I will be able to help her. But Father on the other hand is just about fun and games. He tries to keep Thomas, Mary, John, Samuel, Katherine, Jake, and thou amused while Mum chats with Tamilie and Sindra's mum. Well, that is pretty much all there is to tell you about. All about my parents, that is.

Love always,
Hattie

Dear Diary,

Today the weather has been somewhat for-
giving and Tamilie and I were allowed on the
deck for the first time! It is so long, wide, and
spacious compared to the crowded ways that we
have been living in under the deck. Tamilie and
I happened to catch a glimpse of the passenger
list, and we saw the names of some of the girl
passengers and, of course, their religion. Right
now I don't have the strength to write all of the
names that were on the list. I miss Sindra more
than anyone, even more than the Saulingtons!
You see, I accidentally overheard the Saulingtons
talking and what they said is well unforgivably
sinful! They said something that, I swear, I will
remember as long as I live and I will tell to anyone who has the slightest notion to ask! They
said that they were glad that she fell overboard
because it was an innocent way of death to
strike! They said that she was a worthless child

and that they were planning on having another one as soon as they reach the new land so that it looks like they were mourning all that time and they figure that by then people won't suspect about how gay and joyous they have been all this time! I disagree with the Saulingtons completely. Sindra did most of the woman work and was more useful than her indolent mother! I must go now because I am afraid that if I do anything more that my rage will tempt me to tear out all the pages in this blasted diary and give them to the blasted sea!

> Sincerely,
> Hattie

October 26, 1620
Early Afternoon, *Mayflower*

Dear Diary,

Today Mother and I made fifty fresh loaves of bread! We started at 5:30 A.M. and we just now finished at 4:30! I hear that the Dutch buy everything from England and the fashions and furniture are going to be imported all the way from good old England! I trust that will cost a bundle! Oh, how I wish I was Dutch. With all the fancies of England, the frills of their dresses to the silk fabric of the bonnets. Oh, how lucky some girls are to be born Dutch. Why couldn't I have been born Dutch?

Sincerely,
Hattie

October 27, 1620
Evening, *Mayflower*

Dear Diary,

Today I lost my church dress! I have looked and looked all over the place for it, but I can't find it anywhere. It is terribly dreadful. And my mum has punished me a horrible punishment. I am not allowed to have dinner for two whole weeks! But I still have to stand behind my parents with my brothers and sisters as if I were eating. That is so that I, too, will punish myself for losing my dress by watching everyone else eat delicious foods. Tonight my mum deliberately served my favorite dish. They had porridge, bread, and three pieces of pork to the children and five to the adults. I was not even allowed in the conversations that were taking place. All this just because of a stupid, old, and plain church dress.

Grrrrrr.

> Sincerely,
> Hattie

> October 29, 1620
> Morning, *Mayflower*

Dear Diary,

Today there is a fine breeze and the salt water is blown into misty drops that are quite refreshing once they hit your back. or when it hits your face and blows your bonnet off into the sea to float away like a ship forever. Today was the first warm day, but the captain says we'll be lucky if it lasts past noon. Tamilie and I went out on the deck and looked over the edge only to see ourselves in the dark waters below us. That is when Tamilie's bonnet fell down into the sea and she, too, was punished but, of course, not as severe as me 'cause she didn't lose her church dress but her bonnet. She has to go one week without lunch. Although we both got a whipping on our other end for looking so far over the edge. I suppose, though, that we deserved it. But don't tell Tamilie, but I think so!

Flagellation
Scouring
Castigation
Flogging

In case you're wondering, Tamilie and I decided that we should both write down other words that mean the same thing as whipping to help us take our mind off how long we won't be able to sit down! By the way, what do you think of my list?
     Sincerely,
     Hattie

November 6, 1620
Morning, *Mayflower*

Dear Diary,

I am dreadfully bored today. You see, the weather is unbearably cold and wet so everyone is cooped up down below deck. Mum is convinced that since the weather is abhorrent, loathsome, and abominable that I should help her cook for everyone! I just can't stand it! Thou should have never left England. I could have been adopted by a wealthy family and dressed in frills and silk. With bonnets of silk and shoes of leather, oh, how marvelously splendid and luxurious it would all have been. Then other Puritan girls who hated being Puritans would be envious of me! Little old me. Who would of thought that anyone would be envious of me? Well, I've got to be going now for my mum wants me to help her with the delicious dinner that I won't even be able to eat.

Sincerely,
Hattie

November 6, 1620
Evening, *Mayflower*

Dear Diary,

Tonight little Mary got sick, and she went to bed burning hot. So hot that it hurt to even touch her and yet she complained of being cold all blasted night. How can that be? She is burning hot and yet she is cold at the same time? I don't understand out of all the other children in my family I have never seen anything quite like this. And guess who has to stay up all night with the child. It is so inquisitive.

Sincerely,
Hattie

November 8, 1620
Late Morning, *Mayflower*

Dear Diary,

There has been some sort of outbreak, and people are hot and cold at the same time. They also cough up blood. They have labeled it as TB. Mum is scared that Mary won't live to see the

New World and she doesn't want to lose another child. She said that it just hurts too much. Oh, I'm sorry you don't know about Emily. You see Emily was born two years after I was, but she died at the age of four. She died of smallpox three days before Thomas was born and one year after Katherine was born. That year we all dressed plainer than before and we all wore black. People brought us food and cards to show their sorrow, too, of little Emily.

November 10, 1620
Morning, *Mayflower*

Dear Diary,

Several men have died, leaving poor young women as widows coming into this New World. The source of their death was TB, which makes Mum fear every day about Mary. Mary coughs up blood every day. Never stopping. It is horrible watching her lie there helpless. I want to go over there and hug her or at least tell her a story or tell about what is being said above the *Mayflower*. All she ever smells is the smell of blood, spew, phlegm, and dirty diapers — not ever one whiff of fresh air. The poor dear. Well I must be going now for I am afraid that I will cry and stain the only paper that I have.

Love,
Hattie

November 16, 1620
Evening, *Mayflower*

Dear Diary,

Today the morning is dull and not a bit of sun peeks through the cracks in the worn wood. Mum is more depressed then ever. As you already know that Mary has TB, well, we have just learned that Thomas has the blooming illness also. It is horrible. It's simply horrible. I fear that if Mum loses both Mary and Thomas that she shall break down in a stage of folly and sit around all day while Father tries to comfort her and take care of the other children at the same time. All this will be happening while I am off in a dream that has come true. A dream that I have wanted ever since I was a little girl and will finally have while my mum is being folly. Thomas is only in the beginning stage of TB, but so far he doing worse than Mary is now. This whole epidemic is terribly dreadful and tiring. Every time that Mary and Thomas go to sleep, we all hold our breath in fear that they are going to sleep. Well, actually we all hold our breath in fear that they will never wake up, that they will take their last breath and say adieu. It is time for us to all shut our eyes and sleep for the night is long but the days are much longer. I will now say a prayer and cover myself in thou's blankets, shut my eyes, and dream.

Love always,
Hattie

November 20, 1620
Morning, *Mayflower*

Dear Diary,

Today is quite gloomy and everyone groans about how confoundedly cramped we all are. Every night I feel the breath of Katherine on my neck. Although there is one advantage and that is that it is easier to stay warm. Tamilie and I are cooped up in this blasted ship all day, and we never get a breath of fresh air. Mr. William Blythe and his wife, Antoinette Marie Blythe, and their daughter, Whitney Gwyndlen Blythe, are the richest people on this blasted ship, and they have a special machine that a famous inventor in England gave them. It allows them to capture air of any sort and it supposedly turns it into fresh air. Tamilie and I wish we were in the Dutch Cluth Club that the rich Dutch girls are in. But it is impossible because naturally the only girls that are allowed in it are the Dutch.

Sincerely,
Hattie

November 21, 1620
Morning, *Mayflower*

Dear Diary,

Today the rain splashes the deck of the tumbling ship. The wind is punching us with its hard fist of perish and causes screams when it sneaks up on us. The Snalter boys are sacrificing their lives by going up on deck to patch the sail with their own shirts. Johnathan Snalter is in love with Whitney Blythe. But that is no surprise. All the young men on the ship are in love with Whitney Blythe. Oh, how I wish all the young men on the *Mayflower* adored me. Well, maybe not all the men but at least Johnathan. I must be the ugliest girl on the ship, even Tamilie is prettier then I am. But Whitney Blythe is definitely without a doubt the most gorgeous girl on the ship. She has light red hair with beautiful curls that flow down her shoulders. She has green eyes and freckles on her nose that goes slightly on to her eye bone. She isn't too skinny but at the same time she is not at all fat. The way she looks is perfect. She's beautiful but yet cute at the same time. Oh, how I wish that I were Whitney Gwyndlen Blythe. Ahhh.

Sincerely,

Hattie

Dear Diary,

Today our sail was struck by lightning, and we all had to bring buckets of water to help the fire die down. But I must tell you that it was quite beautiful. Vibrant colors of oranges and yellows with blue water splashing like a splotch on a dress. Although things didn't look so beautiful to everyone. Mrs. Campbell's husband died in the fire along with a great deal of our sail. You see he was walking back from pushing water, when Mr. Chamber wasn't paying attention to what he was doing and pushed a tremendous amount of water onto Mr. Campbell's body and flung him back into a hungry fire. I believe that I will always remember Mrs. Campbell's expression. Her chunky peach-colored cheeks were now white and had tears rolling down them gently. Later Mum and I made her hot tea and allowed her to cry as long has she wanted. But she didn't because Mary began dragging herself out of our sleeping room. She was as white as a ghost and had blood dribbling down her lips. Mum cried for Father, and Mrs. Campbell immediately dried her tears and tried to help in any way that she could while I stood there blankly in shock over the horrible scene. Pa rushed in with a flushed look. When he saw Mary, he took a step backward and then several forward. He cried at me to go and get the doctor. At first I did nothing, I just stood there staring at my sister. I tried to move but I couldn't. My body was frozen. The only thing I could move was my eyes. I suddenly felt a cold brisk breeze as Pa walked by me frantically. I suppose he got tired of waiting for me and he went to get the doctor himself. My body felt as if it had just been hit with hundreds of icy, cold knives. Was I dead? I couldn't tell. Right then and there I fainted and fell onto the ground. The rest was just a blank. All I could feel was icy pricks that kept touching my body. They never stopped. My head was throbbing. I woke up to find the docter sitting by me feeling my body and the tremendous lump on my head. His cool fingers chilled my body. In the background I could hear my mother crying faintly, but her face was nothing but a blur. Mary had died minutes before. Pa wasn't crying. He was trying to be brave. And he succeeded, although I heard him at night crying by himself. The darkness smothers him to the point where I can barely see his outline. I am the only one who hears and I shall keep it that way.

Love always,
Hattie

November 27, 1620
Evening, *Mayflower*

Dear Diary,

The days seem to be getting longer and longer. Instead of feeling like we're getting closer to the New World, it feels like every day we keep getting farther and farther away from it. Well, I must be going for I haven't been well for the last few days and I don't to make myself worse.

Sincerely,
Hattie

November 30, 1620
Afternoon, *Mayflower*

Dear Diary,

The days are much colder and darker now than they were before. The great winds howl and moan all night long. Thunder stretches across the sky trying to attack us with cannon-balls. It is almost Christmas, and I have been busy making Tamilie and my siblings dolls, scarves, hats, and mittens. Mum is doing this exact thing except only for her children. Even Pa is making presents for each of us. More and more people are dying of TB every day, and I can't help but think of Mary my dear sister. People are still bringing bread and other goods for us. Even the Blythes have brought several loaves of bread!

Sincerely,
Hattie

December 2, 1620
Morning, *Mayflower*

Dear Diary,

Everybody is quite frantic that the celebration of Christ's birth may be wrecked by all the sickness that has recently come about. People will be fine one day and the next they will be coughing up blood all over the ship. That is all that we smell. Blood, phlegm, and dirty air. It always reeks, and the sad thing is that everyone is unfortunately getting used to it! Even babies are catching this deadly sickness. It is a wonder that thou doesn't get sick with the smell of sickness in the air.

Sincerely,
Hattie

December 6, 1620
Morning, *Mayflower*

Dear Diary,

Every day now this ship sneaks us closer and closer to the "New World." I overheard the captain and crew about reaching the "New Land" in about ten days! This is very exciting news. Tamilie and I both want to be Dutch, but we don't know how we will both be doing it without looking too obvious. I'm going to make it seem as though Indians have captured me as if I have "disappeared." I will then change my identity and become Dutch. We are still trying to think up a plan for Tamilie. My mother seems as though we are all going to die because Mary left us. Father tries to convince us that things will be just fine as long as we don't lose one more child. Does that mean that if I become Dutch, they will all die? I suppose I am being quite selfish. I can't help it. It has always been my dream to be Dutch. Just like this was Father's dream to come to the New World, and he got it. He even dragged us all along. At least I'm not making my family become Dutch. It's all Father's fault that Mary died if we hadn't taken this voyage on this confounded ship. Mary would still be alive. When my dream comes true, no one will lose his or her life!

Sincerely,
Hattie

Dear Diary,

More people have been taken ill. Mum doesn't let any of us out onto the deck. I'm surprised that we all don't catch TB from lack of fresh air. Tamilie's brother Peter has got some sort of sickness that no one has heard of. His stomach hurts constantly, and his head is burning rapidly. He has cast all over the place, but he doesn't lose any blood. Mum insists that if we all have to stay belowdeck that our duties should be doubled! When Tamilie's mother heard about this so-called "wonderful" idea, she immediately started all fifteen of her children on doubled work. All except Peter that is.

The oldest boy, Brocke, had quadrupled duties because he had to take over Peter's duties also! Although this is no fun, it keeps us busy, and after we're done, Tamilie and I go and watch the Blythes' entertainment through a small hole in their door. It is quite fun but sometimes we have to leave early or else we might burst out laughing and then the Blythes would catch us looking in a hole through the door. I don't think that would work in our favor. The Blythes' pride and joy is their beautiful daughter, Whitney. Whitney was the only child the Blythes were able to have, and they're trying to find a proper young lady to adopt so that Whitney will always have a playmate or someone to talk to whenever she wants. But they also want it to go deeper than just friendship but into sisterhood. I overheard them talking one day. There is also another Dutch lady that would like to adopt a young girl. Her husband passed away and she only has her four-year-old little girl. Her name is Mrs. Beatu DeCrau. We are hoping that Mrs. DeCrau will adopt Tamilie, and hopefully she will live nearby. Mrs. DeCrau is a stout woman with brown hair and blue eyes. Her hair is always up in a loose bun that is covered by a warm buttermilk bonnet. She doesn't talk much and she is very strict but is also very warm and nice but in her own way. Her husband died about a week ago. He was a kind man who taught us all how to play games. I cried when he died. He never really cared about people being Dutch or Puritan. All that he thought was that we were people just like everyone else. I will never forget that grin that he always wore. Even in the worst of situations he always had something positive to say, and I hope that I will grow up to have that in me, too.

Sincerely,
Hattie

December 12, 1620
Morning, *Mayflower*

Dear Diary,

Every day our long voyage comes closer and closer to an end. It seems as if everything we know will be gone. No winding cobblestone streets to get to Father's silver shop. Just plain old dirty dirt. I have also heard that Indians are not scarce in this country and many of them will kill for no reason at all. The days seem to be getting shorter and shorter, each day leaving less time to prepare for what shall come in this new home. I feel horrible, not ever able to go up onto the deck. But tonight Tamilie and I are going to go up there when no one is around and stay up there as long as we can or until we hear from below. I do hope no one catches us. By the way, Mrs. Contier lost her husband and both of her children two nights ago. She is a very nice young lady of sixteen, and I feel gravely sorry for the poor dear. But I have also heard that the Blythes and she are very good friends and that they are planning on living near one another. Which could be good news for Tamilie and me.

Always,
Hattie

December 14, 1620
Afternoon, *Mayflower*

Dear Diary,

Today has been much better than most of the dreary days have been, and Tamilie and I were allowed to walk all around the ship everywhere except the deck and men's quarters. It was quite exciting! Tamilie and I have roamed around a good part of the ship before but we have never seen the whole ship before. Tamilie and I were and still are quite amazed about how much ship there really is. Although it does make you think how many people could really be on the ship at once, and we didn't even see the men's or crew's quarters.

Sincerely,
Hattie

December 15, 1620
Morning, *Mayflower*

Dear Diary,

It seems that we have been by shore for a month and we never knew because Mum wouldn't let us go on deck.

LAND!!

Sincerely,
Hattie

Dear Diary,

Today they are allowing women and children off the ship! There is a nice girl who is my age who was shoved off a stepping-stone by the ever annoying Johnny and Francis Billington. Oh, how Remember was so mad when she plunged into the water, she was ready to strangle Johnny and Francis. Tamilie and I had to hold her back but we should have let her go after them because Francis and Johnny were lifting up our dresses so that everyone could see our rears! How utterly embarrassing it was. I can never show my face or should I say rear again!

Sincerely,
Hattie

Dear Diary,

The New World is just as I expected: HOR-
RIBLE. There are no shops, no paths unless you
count dirt, which is everywhere, and most of all
there are no *Homes*! I can't believe that Father
would want to move to such a wretched place
such as this. But at least or so I hope I will be living in luxury with Blythes. Tamilie is now un-
sure of becoming Dutch. She complains about
what if they figure out who she is or if her parents recognize her in a crowd. But methinks
Tamilie worries too much and that inside methinks she is a little scared. But with or without
Tamilie, no matter what, I will do it.

Sincerely,
Hattie

Dear Diary,

Today there have been quite violent storms. Wind tears through the rigging. Some Pilgrims be on land with no victuals, or shelters. They hope to put out a shallop to later send in provender and provisions. We have now let down three anchors to ride on now so turbulent be the seas that we sit upon. This turbulence is making everyone sick, and four people have already cast, and the stench has stretched all the way from the men's quarters to the women's and children's quarters! It is unbelievable. Tamilie and I haven't seen each other ever since we walked all over the great ship and it will probably stay that way until we have shelters built. Although Tamilie and I can't see each other that doesn't mean that we can't contrive. We are right next door and so we talk through the little holes in the door. But for some strange reason I think that our mums don't want us to talk ever again. Something is going on around here, but I just can't put my finger on it.

Love,
Hattie

December 23, 1620
Morning, Plimoth Harbor

Dear Diary,

Mistress Allerton, one of the Blythes' close friends, gave birth to a dead son last night. They wrapped him up, put him in a small box, and today we took him ashore to bury him properly. We have all gone ashore today to begin work. Men have begun felling timber to build shelters and eventually shops. I walked around with Father trying to find the most suitable place for our house that I would only live in for a matter of months. Father and I found a nice little patch of land that would be a perfect location for a home. It had millions of trees and a little field in the back. There was one huge hole that had only grass on it and that would be where our house would be built. It is quite a nice site for a house and it would allow us to have more room then most people who are planning to settle here.

Love,
Hattie

December 25, 1620
Afternoon, Plimoth Harbor

Dear Diary,

I have some bad news today. The beautiful site that we were planning to build our house has been taken by a man by the name of Jacob Lemming. He insists that Father didn't claim the land, therefore the land was not anyone's and anyone could have claimed it. We were not anticipating this, so we have no backup plan. Which means that we got stuck with a dumpy little site of land that could barely hold a house that had two rooms in it! It is just a bunch of clumps of mud that make your feet sink into the ground and give you a struggle when you try to pull them out. Why did we have to get stuck with such a dump?

Sincerely,
Hattie

December 29, 1620
Morning, Plimoth Harbor

Dear Diary,

Today is quite wet and cold. My nose keeps turning a violent color red, and I can't feel my fingers. There is a storm brewing in the gloomy sky, and the site for our house is nothing but a big puddle. Father says that there is no way that he will be able to build our house here if the weather keeps this up. People are sore to go to work, but at least they actually have land to work with instead of a big puddle of dirty water. From the decks of the *Mayflower* I can see big columns of smoke rising into the air from the Indian fires. I can only hope that they are a distance away. I still haven't seen an Indian yet and I hope to keep it that way.

> Sincerely,
> Hattie

December 30, 1620
Morning, Plimoth Harbor

Dear Diary,

More stormy weather. Too powerful and beastly for the men to work. Mum is very tired and tries to rest as often as possible. But with my rambunctious siblings it is nearly impossible. One of us always needs something. I try to keep Katherine entertained, but it is quite difficult. She is always pretending to be my mother and me her baby, but she always insists on carrying me until we both tumble to the floor and she goes off crying to Mum and I'm left with a bruised something or other.

> Love,
> Hattie

January 1, 1621
Evening, Plimoth Harbor

Dear Diary,

The year hath turned and I now write a numeral for the present year on this glorious page. It seems as though this was the wrong time to leave for this hard task. Perhaps if we had waited in Holland for another year and then left in the spring of 1621, it wouldn't be such a difficult task as to build a shelter. We would arrive in the summer, and the land would be dry. No mud puddles, no sopping wet grass, and no numb body parts. How much more enjoyable it would have been. But what is done is done and nothing can change what is done. Who knows?

Sincerely,

Hattie

January 2, 1621
Plimoth Harbor

Dear Diary,

Today my siblings and I took a stick and made figures in the mud as to play Scotch Hoppers. We played for a long while until Mum started calling to us for getting our clothes dirty. We went into the ship drenched, dirty, and guilty. Mum scolded us all, especially me, and for punishment we have to stay in our clothes like so all day long. All except Katherine that is.

Sincerely,
Hattie

January 3, 1621
Morning, Plimoth Harbor

Dear Diary,

Today is my birthday, but unfortunately my family is too busy working that there will be no celebration. Today is the day that one year ago I received you. Mum had been making you for a week now, and I had never suspected that you were for me. I was so thrilled that I cried because parchment is so very expensive. But this year there will be no present, and no one will remember that my birthday went on without anyone knowing. The only people who even acknowledge that today is my birthday are Katherine, Tamilie, and me. Not even my own mother remembers, and she was there at the birth.

Love,
Hattie

January 3, 1621
Evening, Plimoth Harbor

Dear Diary,

Guess what! I have some terrific news. Everyone did remember my birthday. It was supposed to be a surprise. Mum and Katherine made me two gingerbread cookies, Katherine made me a card, and Mum and Father bought me a new quill and ink! And my last present was a brand-new church dress that Mum made from wool she had brought from England that she was going to use in case of emergencies. As I looked up at my loving family, I cried and cried as I thought that in a matter of mere months I would betray them. Betray the people who loved me and all that I could do was run into my living chambers in the *Mayflower.*

Love,
Hattie

January 6, 1621
Afternoon, Plimoth Harbor

Dear Diary,

Today the weather screams and howls. The rain blasts and spatters the deck and makes loud ping noises. The racket carries to under deck and makes children, especially babies, cry. Father is outside trying to find a way to patch up the holes on the site where we plan to live. He has come inside several times swearing that there is no way we will be able to live there. Mum settles him down with a hot cup of tea, and Katherine continuously draws pictures on a scrap of slate that she found somewhere. He returns outside calm and comes back in sopping and anxious. It has been going on this way for several hours now.

Love,

Hattie

January 16, 1621
Afternoon, Plimoth Harbor

Dear Diary,

Today the weather is as turbulent as usual. It is getting so boring only seeing rain and feeling wind. Twice I felt as though I was going to catch the wind and blow off with it! Tamilie and I still don't see each other much, and we hardly talk unless we happen to bump into each other and have the courtesy to apologize. I miss having a friend to talk to. I wonder if Tamilie feels the same. I hope so, because that would mean that we would still have a chance of becoming friends again.

Love always,

Hattie

January 20, 1621
Evening, Plimoth Harbor

Dear Diary,

Mum and I have had a horrendous fight, and we haven't spoken to each other in days. All I did was ask her why it seems as though Tamilie and I have been forbidden to see each other and she began to yell furiously at me and told me that it was none of my business. Well that got me so mad because it was my business. Tamilie and I were best friends, and I slapped my mum right across her face with all my might! Her face had a big red slap mark left across it. I was so upset after I realized what I had done that I broke out in tears and tried to beg for her forgiveness. But it didn't work. All she could do was stare at me and there we stayed as though we were painted on a canvas until finally Mummy walked away. Now all I can think about is what a horrible child I am. What kind of dignified person would slap her very own mum?

Love,
Hattie

Dear Diary,

Today I woke up groggier then ever. The coldness has numbed my body to the point where it hurts to move my fingers the slightest bit! Mum still doesn't talk to me, but I guess it is only right that she shan't. Tamilie and I still don't talk, but now I think that it has gone further than our parents forbidding for now every time we walk near each other she gives me dirty looks and continues on talking to either her mum or a new Puritan friend. If you ask me, I think that she is doing it on purpose, trying to get me jealous, but it isn't working. Well, not completely. Instead I ignore her and talk to my new friends Remember or Mem or Hummy. They are much better friends than Tamilie ever was and they are much better than Tamilie ever will be. Oh, but how I miss her so. Only one thing ponders me and that is why does she hate me so as she does? If only I knew, then my awe would be disstupe-factioned and I wouldn't ponder all day even when I was with Hummy and Mem. I know that this makes probably no sense, and I understand that as this is not making complete sense to me, either, but this is what they call the time of making no sense and I indeed am succeeding in that. Thank you for listening anyway.

Sincerely,
Hattie

January 31, 1621
Afternoon, Plimoth Harbor

Dear Diary,

The tremendous winds roar and howl making it almost impossible to sleep at night. Every once in a while the rain seeps through some of the little cracks and drips on me, which hits my body like a thousand knives stabbing you all at once with shrieks of pain. This only adds to my numbness. Mum has finally given in and now talks to me because of Mary. Mary reminds her that she is dead and how sad Mum would be if she lost another child. Mum came in last night and gave a great hug and kiss that symbolizes forgiveness. I was so happy that we had made up that I got up bright and early at 4:00 and busied myself in making breakfast for everyone! Father goes out every day trying to work on our soon to be house. But every night he comes back in drenched, cursing, and chilled to the bone. Mum tries to warm him up, and every morning she begs of him not to go outside today, but he is too stubborn to listen and says that if he doesn't do it every day he'll just keep putting it off and it will never get done. It goes on like this every day and night. Mum is so exhausted every day that I fear that she will collapse on the spot! Sometimes I feel as though I am not doing enough and that I should do more of Mum's work. Mum disagrees completely and tells me to go and entertain my brothers and sisters but it is very hard with such a rambunctious group of children in such a small area of room. There are just too many of us.

Sincerely,
Hattie

Dear Diary,

Today is Tamilie's birthday, and there will be
no celebration that I was invited to. I wonder if
I should give her the present I made for her during this horrendous journey. Would that make
her like me once more or would she turn around
in disgust at the sight of me before I had a
chance to give it to her? What could I have pos-
sibly done that would cause such great harm
and damage to our friendship? Sure, Mem and
Hummy are nice but they just aren't what I had
with Tamilie. I don't think that I will ever have
such a great friendship with anyone like this one.
Tamilie and I are — er — were so very tight
how could I ever have another friendship as perfect as ours was? Well, maybe you could wish her
a happy fifteenth birthday because I wasn't invited.

Sincerely,

Hattie

Dear Diary,

It seems as though Tamilie did have a celebration but only for her closest friends. I nearly started crying when I found out. But something very funny entered my mind. I suddenly realized that Tamilie is enormous! She has been getting fatter and fatter! Instead of crying, all I could do was laugh, and I laughed so hard that my eyes began to water and I fell down laughing on the floor until I couldn't laugh any longer. Mem and Hummy looked at me as though I were folly. I suppose, though, that it was quite interesting to see me laugh like I did and about my ex-best friend's party. I realized why they had thought that I was drunk and I told them why I had been laughing. Instead of laughing with me they just stared as though they were statues until finally Mem said that she was surprised no one had told me that Tamilie is pregnant! When I heard this, I nearly collapsed. Right then and there I marched down to Tamilie's living chambers and asked her why she had never told me. Apparently her mum had told my mum that she thought that I would never get married and my mum said well at least my child has the dignity to get married before she gets pregnant and that is when Tamilie was forbidden to see me. Tamilie and I are back to being best friends again and this time we are stronger because we know that we will have to fight our parents to stay friends forever.

Love,
Hattie

March 12, 1621
Morning, Plimoth Harbor

Dear Diary,

I am dreadfully sorry for not writing sooner but things around here have been horrendous. Father just barely finished the house before the *Mayflower* left. We must have been the last ones to depart from the great ship. This house was poorly constructed and Father is already looking for a new site before the new Pilgrims have a chance to settle all the empty land. I suppose I'm luck because today will be my last day here. But it's not as easy as it seems. I'll have to do it in the afternoon. Another concern is how I can ensure the fact that I get the Blythes. Where will I stay? Is there already an orphanage? What will I do if in the woods there really are Indians? Will they scalp me like they did Missy Tiual? I overheard Sir Thomas Barkley talking to Madam Porsh that there have been Indian warnings numerous times and that she should keep her children completely indoors after 12:00 at the latest. He said that he would be telling all the settlers this. Which means that if I want to do this then I have to do it all at 10:30 because when I don't come back after 12:00 Mum will have Father send search parties after me. I know this because last time I was out until 12:15 there were all ready four search parties after me! You are one of the only things I am bringing because I can't bring all my belongings or else it might look a little suspicious. I will write in you once I reach my destination. If we don't talk for a while, then thank you. Thank you for being such a wonderful and reliable friend.

Love always (Dutch or not),
Hattie

March 13, 1621
Morning, Plimoth Harbor

Dear Diary,

I have made it safely so far and now I am trying to strategize, which I don't know very much about because I don't go to school like my brothers. Currently I am in the woods and several times I have heard the whispers of men who are trying to find me. Last night I had begun trying to climb a tree to see if there were any columns of gray smoke. But after about three feet in a hoop skirt my hands slipped off the great tree trunk and I found myself tumbling to the ground. I had landed with a tremendously loud thump and I felt my body aching with my back pounding my chest as though it were bulging. I felt a tingling sensation arise on my back as though a million little needles were pricking my back all at the same time. I smelled a wonderful smell that Father said was pine when I first came off the *Mayflower*. It is quite cold, and my body is even number then it was on the *Mayflower*! I wonder if Mum and Father even miss me. One of the most important belongings of mine that I brought was a small painting of my family that my mum and father had given me in private on my birthday. It was made right before we left Holland. I treasured it more then anything that I had, especially now because I don't have a family anymore.

Love always,
Hattie

March 19, 1621
Morning, Plimoth Harbor

Dear Diary,

More snow. It seems as if every day it snows until many people cannot open their front door. The blasted coldness pierces my body with shocks of pain as if I were lying on millions of puncturing knives and needles. I have found a shelter that takes children in to find homes. They call this situation an orphanage. I can only hope that Mum and Father don't come in here hoping to find a new child to bring home with them. I overheard Miss Paeragrue reading a letter from the Blythes on what kind of child they be wanting. If I'm on my best behavior (which I've tried my best to be on), then I would fit the description perfectly. At the same time I shall have a little competition with Tierra Valentine. She, too, fits the Blythes' description perfectly, but she might have a better chance of them liking her because she is much prettier than I am or ever will be.

Love,
Hattie

April 2, 1621
Afternoon, Plimoth Harbor

Dear Diary,

Bad news. As I thought, Tierra Valentine or should I say Tierra Blythe has won over the hearts of Whitney and Sir Blythe. Miss Paera-grue says that she has another family who might want to adopt me and that family is coming on the sixteenth. Miss Paeragrue is a very kind woman and favors me. She has told me that there is another girl who has been lost in woods for some time now who will be coming out shortly.

Love,
Hattie

April 6, 1621
Evening, Orphanage

Dear Diary,

Good news. Tamilie and I have been re-united. You see, Tamilie was the girl who Miss Paeragrue had been talking about the day be-fore! Jane, a little girl the age of six, has taken to me quite well and now she acts as if I were her older sister. She is adorable. She has red curly hair, green eyes, and slightly peach cheeks. She is already acting as if she were twenty-six! I do hope she can adjust to having Tamilie around also. Tamilie is quite nice but I fear that Jane wants me all to herself. Tamilie has already told me that she thinks Jane is a waif. Well, I must now go for there be a set sleeping time.

Love,
Hattie

April 16, 1621
Morning, Orphanage

Dear Diary,

It seems as though there will be a couple coming to adopt a child today. Miss Paeragrue has made me a new dress and bonnet! They are beautiful yellow and they each have a blue sash! She has helped me curl my hair with pieces of cloth on bath night (which was yesterday). One would almost think I was pretty if they hadn't seen thou before. Well I must be going now for Miss Paeragrue is shouting that the couple is coming down the dirt road.

Love,
Hattie

P.S. I have had to change my name so I changed it to Catherine Georgina Jenkins.

Dear Diary,

Guess what. The couple who was coming to adopt a child sure gave Tamilie and me quite a fright. For, you see, the couple who was coming was my mum and father! They came in and promptly noticed me. Miss Paeragrue introduced all of us. Mum and Father just stood there blankly. Tamilie or should I say Emily Peltina Currie just sat there staring at each other not knowing what to do. Would they tell or would they adopt us? What should we do? But just then Miss Paeragrue came in asking if they had found their "Dream Child." And surprisingly enough they replied quickly without taking their eyes off me yes. And they replied that they wanted Jane! What a relief. But oh, how upset Jane was that they didn't choose me along with her that she nearly refused to go until I gave her my favorite doll and bonnet. She was so thrilled that stopped her crying and she wriggled out a tremendous smile. Thou shall miss her oh, so very much but I know that Tamil-, oops thou means Emily, shan't. One would think that this is funny but I don't think that Mum and Father recognized thou with curly hair and beautiful clothes!

Love always,

Hattie

April 30, 1621
Morning, Orphanage

Dear Diary,

Today the orphanage is cold, damp, and drafty. Miss Paeragrue is busy making a meager breakfast with a biscuit and a small bowl of porridge. It is so cold in here that I wear my shawl. I wear my warmest clothes made out of wool. Miss Paeragrue's flaming red hair now matches her complexion, for she be working so hard. I must go now for it is time to eat breakfast.

Love,

Hattie

Dear Diary,

This morning three Indians came pounding on our orphanage door! Their long black hair was beautiful and was so black that it almost looked green. Their beautiful leather suits had fringe and beads. Their shoes were beautiful but quite funny-looking. They were leather but they had beautiful fur all around them. But I believe that my favorite was his long feather that was tucked softly in his hair. They then knocked on the door once but harshly. Miss Paeragrue promptly opened the door, and the Indians asked if she would be willing to trade extra shirts for the children of their tribe who don't have any for some pairs of moccasins, I think. Miss Paeragrue gladly excepted and within ten minutes they were gone.

Love,
Hattie

May 14, 1621
Afternoon, Orphanage

Dear Diary,

Great news. I have been adopted! Miss Paeragrue has decided to adopt me. Although it was never my dream to live in an orphanage, at least I will know that I have a loving and caring mum. Thou shall always have someone to play with. Miss Paer-, I mean Mum has decided that tomorrow we shall make soap. Which I am quite excited about because I love making soap.

Sincerely,

Hattie

May 15, 1621
Evening, Home

Dear Diary,

Today we had a wonderful time making soap. We made so many that I can't remember them all. My favorite is pink with a rose perfume. Tamilie's or should I say Emily's favorite is orange with lavender. Tomorrow is bath night, and by then we should have enough soap for everyone to have their own. Miss Paeragrue promises to curl Tamilie and thou's hair so that we look beautiful in the morning.

Love always,
Hattie

May 20, 1621
Evening, Home

Dear Diary,

Bad news. Yesterday Tamilie was adopted by a Quaker family and now she lives in a different colony! Thou shall never see her again. We have promised to write every month but I know that that is a promise we both can't keep.

Sincerely,
Hattie

May 25, 1621
Morning, Home

Dear Diary,

Today I got a letter but it was not from Tamilie and thou was quite shocked actually when I read that it was from Tierra Valentine Blythe! She wrote to tell thou that she misses me and I pasted her very letter right in this diary.

Dear Catherine,

    The Blythes are wonderful and I love Whitney as if she really were my very own sister. But I miss you and Miss Paeragrue oh, so much. I felt as if we never always got along and I hope that you don't think that I am some sort of competitive waif. When the Blythes chose me, I was quite happy and stayed that way. One day I even got up the courage to ask them if they would please adopt you. But when they received Miss Paeragrue's letter and found out that you had been adopted, they promptly told me and said that maybe some other time they would adopt another child but for now they shan't. Please write and tell how you be doing.

Love always,

Tierra

When I read this, I felt very sorry about how competitive and mean I was when, in the very end, the person who I was fighting turned out

to be a great friend and I believe that we will always write and stay friends.

Sincerely,

Hattie

Epilogue

Later, Hattie was married to the Blythes' son Johnathan and they had ten children later. Hattie and Tierra stayed close and eventually Hattie told her secret to Tierra only to find out that it didn't matter to her. Tamilie and Hattie never spoke again until Tamilie became dreadfully ill and died the day after Hattie came to visit. Hattie's children grew up to be doctors, lawyers, and housewives. Hattie died in 1689 at the age of eighty-three peacefully in her bed after being a widow for sixteen years. She reunited with Catherine only at her family's funeral after their house caught on fire. Catherine was lucky enough to have been outside. Miss Paeragrue never married and died at the age of thirty-six after the river currents pulled her away to her gloomy death. After that Hattie took over the orphanage, which later the Blythes bought. And that is where this story ends.

About the Author

Of writing *The Journey to a New Land: The Diary of Hattie Simalina Potch*, Sara Doran says, "I chose this particular period of time because we had just begun studying it in school and I found it interesting. It took me approximately six weeks to complete my diary. I wrote at least a little bit every day, first thing in the morning. I enjoyed writing this diary because I love writing and I got really into my story and its characters. I had a lot of fun!

"I love to write! In the second and third grades I had a teacher, Ms. Forsstrom, who encouraged me to write and enter contests. In the third grade I entered a writing contest for the local newspaper. The story had to be a mystery and at least a paragraph long. I wrote about two pages and won! It was the first time my writing had ever been published and I was very excited. I believe that I owe all my writing success to my very supportive family and to Ms. Forsstrom. So I would like to thank them all for everything.

"I love to read! I can usually finish a book in about two or three nights. I think that reading so much gives me a good idea of how to use words. I read mysteries, historical fiction, classics, and, of course, the Dear America books."

Sara Doran is eleven years old and lives in Hillsboro, Oregon. She is the youngest of two children in a family of four. She has three dogs: Rebel, Jasper, and Mick. She is in the fifth grade and this year has been the first year that she has been home-schooled. In addition to being a writer, Sara is a gymnast at the Oregon Gymnastics Academy.

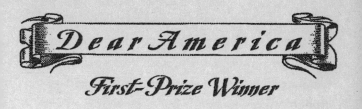

First-Prize Winner

THE DIARY OF
EDWARD DANIEL PHILLIPS

A Union Soldier
Pennsylvania, 1863

BY NATHAN SADASIVAN

Real America

The Quiet History

THE DIARY OF
EDWARD DANIEL PHILLIPS

A Union Soldier
Pennsylvania 1863

By Nathan Sadasivan

Pennsylvania,
1863

Pennsylvania,
1863

June 29, 1863. About 11:00 A.M.
Somewhere North of Taneytown

My name is Edward Daniel Phillips. I am a Union Soldier in the 14th Michigan Regiment, Company D, Army of the Potomac. The journal was Pa's idea, back in March of '61. One month later, I was swept up in the same patriotic fever that so many others were caught in when the Rebels bombed Fort Sumter. At the nearest recruiting post, the youngest age you could be to join up was sixteen, but back then I was only fifteen.

Pa's a lumberman back in Michigan, though, and he wasn't making much money. There are four sisters, two brothers, and me to feed, so when my older brother, John, and I told him that I wanted to join up, he said it was all right. Even still, it took a while to convince him, and it wasn't till July 2 that we started out.

When we finally got there (the nearest recruiting post was at Detroit, and I live about twenty miles away from Detroit), I convinced them that I was sixteen, so I joined up with the 14th. John, who was eighteen then, joined the 3rd Michigan, and he's in Grant's Army of the Tennessee.

It was the 4th of July that I entered the regiment, which seemed to give it special meaning. I signed two-year enlistment papers, thinking that the war would be over in a matter of months. But so far, Robert E. Lee, the Confederate general, whom we call Bobby Lee, has won every single battle he's fought. In fact, now, after two years of us unsuccessfully attacking them, Bobby Lee is invading the North!

There are five days left in my enlistment term, and if the Army of the Potomac hasn't won any victories by then, I am not going to reenlist.

Same Day. Sometime Around Noon
Same Place

About fifteen minutes ago, we received word to pack up and march. Colonel Racker, the regimental commander, gave us half an hour to pack up our things. Lieutenant Thompson, the commander of Company D, gave us twenty-five minutes to get our things ready, because he guessed it would take about five minutes to join with the rest of the regiment.

Anyway, Johnny Thompson, the lieutenant's son, and I are all ready. Johnny's my best friend and only friend here in the army. We both are somewhat alike. We have dark black hair, brown eyes, and both are a little bit shy. Johnny's family came from a farm south of Detroit, just next to the Michigan-Ohio border. For some reason, both his mother and father have blond hair, but his hair is black.

Talking about Michigan reminds me of my home. We weren't rich enough to go to school, but Pa taught me arithmetic, and Ma taught me spelling and reading. I wasn't too keen on mathematics problems, but after a couple years of spelling, I could spell mostly any word that Ma gave me, and I just loved to read. Each day, as soon as my chores were done, I would get out one of the four books that we owned. I probably read each one over at least five times! Oh, that's our bugle call to get into line! I'd better be going.

Same Day. 11:07 P.M.
Somewhere North of Emmitsburg

I am writing this by a small flicker of candle-light. According to Johnny's pocket watch, seven minutes ago the drummers called taps. That's the drumbeat that's supposed to mean lights out, but I just had to write in my journal, and Johnny, who is also my tent mate, said he didn't mind.

At our night roll call, Lieutenant Thompson said that a certain General Buford, in charge of two cavalry brigades, is guarding a small town and is hollering for reinforcements. John Reynolds, the commander of the I, XI, and III Corps is hurrying them along in order to reinforce Buford. The 14th is part of the I Corps, and the I Corps is the first one in line. The lieutenant also said that Joseph Hooker, the army's previous commander in chief, has been replaced with a new commander, George Meade. I didn't really like General Hooker very much, but I'm not fond of this General Meade, either.

Just before we went to our tents, I asked the lieutenant: "What's the name of the town Buford was protecting?" He said: "It doesn't really make a difference, I'll tell it to you anyway. The town's name is Gettysburg."

July 1. 7:30 A.M.
A Peach Orchard, Two Miles South of Gettysburg

I have never been so exhausted in my whole life! Last night, Karl Malz, the camp mischief maker, and his buddies paid no attention to roll call, taps, or tattoo, which is the signal to get up and go to morning roll call. They stayed up all night, shouting, screaming, and laughing. Malz himself is pretty big, and I guess he thought that no one would try to stop them. Around 5:00 A.M., Colonel Racker, Lieutenant Thompson, Sergeant Rice, Sergeant Emath, Corporal Unda, and a couple of army regulars with Sharp's Rifles showed up and finally forced Malz's gang to go to their tents, and temporarily arrested Malz. I don't know what happened, but they brought him back a moment ago.

We're taking a brief rest, but afterward, we're going to continue marching. As a song goes, "Tramp, Tramp, Tramp, the Boys Are Marching!" Unfortunately, it isn't half as happy as the song seems to depict it. Twenty miles a day is, according to military standards, an extremely short distance. Once in a while we have to do forced marches, which can go as long as a hundred miles a day! The first day we did a long march, we covered only five miles in an hour. Even still, some men were so tired that they completely emptied a well in five minutes. I'm not looking forward to this, and I have a feeling the officers are going to push us hard.

Same Day. 9:00 A.M.
A Valley Surrounded by Ridges

My prediction about the officers pressing us hard turns out to be wrong. We are going slowly, sending skirmishers far ahead, followed by snipers, I think that we are very near the battle, even though I cannot see or hear anything to justify this guess.

The terrain around me is very interesting. To the north is a small hill, at the top of which is Gettysburg. North of Gettysburg is a very tall hill that Lieutenant Thompson says is called Oak Hill. To the northwest is a hill called Cemetery Hill because of the cemetery at its summit. East of where we are resting is a long but not very high ridge, the name of which I am not sure. Southwest of me are two hills: a smaller, rocky hill, and a larger, wooded hill. To the west is the Warfield Ridge, and beyond that are Pitzer's Woods.

It looks like excellent ground to fight a battle on, but I'm not very sure that a battle really is

going on. I think I'm going to go ask the lieutenant.

Same Day. A Couple Minutes Later
Same Place

The lieutenant was sitting on his horse some
distance ahead of us. When I asked him my
question, he smiled at me and answered: "A battle's definitely going on, and we will soon be in
the thick of it!" Just then, as if to confirm his
theory, we heard a loud, bone-chilling scream,
which could only be the infamous Rebel yell.
This was followed by the booming of cannons
and the popping and crackling of musketfire.
When I asked Lieutenant Thompson why we
hadn't heard it earlier, he said that from where
he was sitting, he could hear it going on all the
time, and that probably one side or the other had
been pushed back. After this happened, it would
take a while for the Rebs to renew their attack.

Satisfied, I returned. Despite all this, I hope
one part of the lieutenant's prediction *won't* be

correct: that we would be in the thick of the fighting.

Same Day. 10:30 A.M.
Cemetery Hill

Half an hour ago the I Corps arrived on the scene of battle. Two tired brigades of cavalry, equipped with carbines, were firing with all the firepower they had at what turned out to be Henry Heth's Infantry Division. The situation was extremely desperate. To add on to the confusion and delay, somewhere down the line an officer stopped the troops.

We waited for several minutes, as officers rode by, and men hauled and drove artillery trains and supply wagons by. Finally, Colonel Racker appeared, along with another officer who wore the stars of a major general. As we walked off, Lieutenant Thompson whispered that the general who was with Colonel Racker was General Buford. He commanded the cavalry brigades that were fighting Henry Heth.

Just then, another important officer rode by, General John Reynolds himself! Out in the middle of the battle, this dashing officer, riding back and forth, can easily inspire you to make even the most impossible charge.

Reynolds turned toward the lieutenant, and asked what regiment we were from Lieutenant Thompson responded proudly that we were from the 14th Michigan. Reynolds nodded and said that we were being kept in reserve on Cemetery Hill. Malz and a couple others kept quiet until Reynolds rode off, but as soon as he was gone they started groaning and complaining that they didn't get to join the fight. Actually, as far as I'm concerned, we can sit out as reserves as long as possible, but my opinion isn't that of the entire company.

Now we're sitting here, watching the battle. The fighting seems the goriest on the ridge closest to Gettysburg, because it's out in the open. From almost half a mile away, the dead bodies don't seem very bloody, for it is much too far to see the gruesome details. By far the worst part of it is the smell of dead horse! We've tried everything, from digging a wall to covering our noses to looking for some sort of cover, but the smell keeps on getting to us.

The actual fighting has moved out of sight, covered by trees. As soon as Melstner's Iron Brigade clambered up to the top of the closest ridge, the Confederates retreated to the next ridge, which is covered by woods. Next, Cutler's 2nd Brigade charged forward, ushered into battle by John Reynolds. The Rebs tried to withdraw, but a charge made by the Iron Brigade turned that into a disorganized retreat. The Iron Brigade, followed by Cutler's Brigade, chased the Confederates into the woods.

Lieutenant Thompson is pushing his way to the front of the company, and I think that he's going to make an announcement. I'd better put this away and listen.

Same Day. Noon
Same Place

John Reynolds is dead! At about 10:45 a courier rode up to the regiment and told the bad news to the first officer he saw, which turned out to be Lieutenant Thompson. The lieutenant said that Reynolds was urging the 2nd Brigade onward when he was killed. The brigade was starting to dawdle and slow down, so Reynolds rode up to hurry them on. His presence was met by cheers, and some of the men surged forward toward a group of Rebel sharpshooters. Just then the second line of men came up. As they neared the sharpshooters, they slowed down and Reynolds shouted: "Forward! For God's sake, forward!" No sooner had he finished saying these words than a sharpshooter's bullet caught him in the neck and killed him. Abner Doubleday is now in command of the corps.

As soon as the lieutenant finished, there was a period of silence until the lieutenant went off to tell Colonel Racker what had happened. We went back to what we had been doing before (which for me was just sitting around and thinking), but we were much quieter than before. I don't think the I Corps will ever be the same without Reynolds.

Same Day. 12:30 P.M.
Same Place

Just as I opened this journal, Lieutenant Thompson walked by and suggested: "You should make a map of the area." I think that that is a good idea, so I'm going to draw one, based on what I can see. The lieutenant says that he'll help me with the names of some places.

The XI Corps has arrived, and is rushing to the top of Oak Hill. Coming from the north is yet another large body of Confederates. The XI is mostly Dutch, and some question their loyalty after they were routed at Chancellorsville. I say that it's simply chance that old Stonewall Jackson hit them hard. If any other corps had been in their place, that corps would have run, too. Anyway, we'll see just how loyal they are before the day is over.

Same Day. 6:30 P.M.
Same Place

The way that this bullet hole got into my journal is a very long story. It all started out as the XI Corps was rushing up to the top of Oak Hill. The few Rebs that were up there quickly dashed off at the sight of an entire corps charging up the hill at them. As soon as they got up to

the top, the officers started riding around, getting their men into position. Just then, they heard loud screams and shouts, and before they knew it, the Rebels were charging their rear. But instead of fighting it out, those Dutchmen simply dropped their weapons and ran. In a few minutes, the Confederates were swarming over the hill. The I Corps Iron Brigade, along with Cutler's 2nd Brigade, had driven the Confederates in the woods back, and were actually attacking the few remaining Rebs, when the stream of

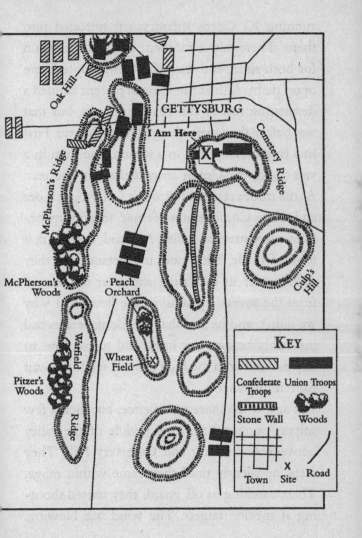

Oak Hill

GETTYSBURG

I Am Here

Cemetery Ridge

McPherson's Ridge

McPherson's Woods

Peach Orchard

Culp's Hill

Warfield

Wheat Field

Pitzer's Woods

Ridge

KEY

Confederate Troops

Union Troops

Stone Wall

Woods

Town

Site

Road

running XI Corps Infantrymen retreated into them. There was a moment of wild confusion for both sides, and then the Confederates were upon them. At first the Unions present handed a devastating fire to the charging Rebs, but that was before they were charged from the rear. First in a tiny trickle, then in a stream, and then in a vast flood, the Union army dashed for the rear. As the troops retreated through Gettysburg more and more Confederates seemed to pop up behind every street and alley. As I said, I'm not that fond of battle, but I can't understand why they didn't order us to charge and clear the snipers from the streets. I just asked the lieutenant why we didn't, and he said that the Confederates had inevitably broken our lines, and so we have to stay put and hold the high ground while we wait for reinforcements.

For a while there was silence, but then a few snipers came out into the middle of the valley between Gettysburg and Cemetery Hill. They crept up silently until they came within range. Then, catching us off guard, they started shooting at specific targets. The wind was blowing, and it was turning the pages of this book. At the precise moment that the last page was directly in the air, the first bullet tore through the bottom left corner of the page. Luckily, the bullet whizzed off to the side. It was a narrow escape, and I immediately shut the book and threw myself flat on the ground. As we were all dashing for cover, Corporal Unda was shot in the arm. Even still, he threw himself behind a big oak tree and bore the pain until the snipers left. After that he started screaming: "Get me an ambulance! For God's sake, get me an ambulance or I'll die!" Some men took him away on a stretcher.

We ate dinner in silence, for there was one less face present. We all wonder whether Corporal Unda will come out just fine, or whether they'll have to amputate his arm, or worse. I am particularly gloomy, for the Confederates have won yet another victory. At this rate, I *definitely* am not going to reenlist!

July 2. Cemetery Ridge
Noon

Early this morning, a courier rode up and told us that we were being moved to the long ridge south of Cemetery Hill. The ridge is simply called Cemetery Ridge. We are right next to Hancock's II Corps, and there is a small stone wall protecting us. General Hancock is quite an inspiring general, partly because during a fight he himself will lead his men and will stay there in the thick of it.

Despite being a little reluctant, we got up and moved to the ridge. We've had breakfast here, and in a few minutes we are going to have lunch here. Because we were reserves and we were being moved to the front of the line, we expected the enemy to make a determined assault in a matter of minutes. All that happened, though, was that a few enemy cannons fired some shells at us, but the Reb artillerymen aren't very good shots, and the shells simply fell into the valley between Gettysburg and Cemetery Ridge.

About an hour ago, something happened that

very much distresses Captain Abraham, Lieutenant Thompson, and most of all Colonel Racker. For me it is very much on the contrary, and I think that it's rather impressive. General Sickles, in charge of the Union III Corps, was ordered to bring his corps to the south to protect Hancock's left flank, and to occupy the two small hills south of Cemetery Ridge. But Sickles decided that that it would be impossible to defend the small valley between Cemetery Ridge and the two hills. In order to cover this valley, Sickles ordered his corps forward. It was quite a sight to see. Ten thousand veteran troops advancing out into the open in grand array. The green-clad snipers went first, followed by the large bodies of blue-clad infantry, grouped into battalions. Their rifles were shouldered jauntily, and they carried themselves with such pride that it seemed nothing could stop them.

Colonel Racker says that if the Confederates attack, they can easily shatter Sickles's position, or "salient" as he calls it. He thinks that because Sickles is a mile in front of Hancock, then that means the Confederates can easily destroy his position because it is to hard to reinforce. If Sickles retreats, then Hancock's II Corps cannot hold out, and it will be up to us to stop them. Colonel Racker says all this despite the fact that it appears that there are no Confederates at all in the Pitzer's Woods, the woods facing Sickles. Even beyond the woods, there is nothing at all but a few wagons and their teamsters. Facing Culp's and Cemetery Hills are many Rebels, and it is obvious that they are going to attack. It would make sense to say that the entire Rebel Army is going to attack the northern flank of ours. But anyway, we will see.

Same Day. 4:00 P.M.
The Summit of the Little Round Top

Not too long ago, Colonel Racker sent me out here to observe Sickles's exact movements. He intends to learn just how bad Sickles is doing, and has lent me his pocket watch, and expects me to report back by 7:00. As soon as I got to the bottom of Cemetery Ridge, the first place I thought of going to was the small rocky hill I now know is called Little Round Top.

I learned this from an officer by the name of G. K. Warren, who is Meade's top Topographical Engineer. He is up here with a crew of signalmen and a cannon. Warren also seems worried about the Confederates attacking Sickles.

Sickles is, at the moment, deploying the two divisions in his corps. His 1st Division, under David Birney, moved onto a small rise with a wheat field to the left and a peach orchard to the right. Birney's line stretched out in between these two landmarks. To the right of Birney is a division under Alexander Humphreys. His line stretches from the peach orchard to the northern end of the rise.

With all the officers worried that Sickles's position is going to be shattered by the Rebels, there may be something to it. But as I said earlier, we will see.

Same Day. 5:30 P.M.
Summit of the Little Round Top

What a fool I am, thinking that Sickles is invincible! Perhaps it was his arrogance that tricked me, but Sickles is doomed now. I have enclosed a map to show the officers back at the regiment.

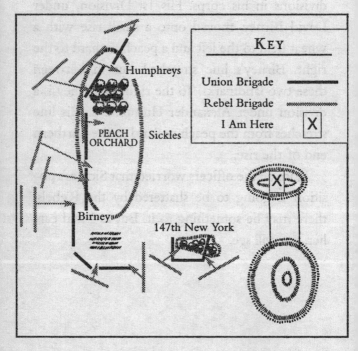

At precisely five o'clock, I don't know how many cannons went off, all at the same time. It seemed like a million sheets of flame, all falling on Sickles's line at the same time. The Confederates didn't even wait a moment for the III Corps to recover. They just rushed forward. For a moment a high-pitched scream — the Rebel yell, echoed throughout the valley. Then, charging from the south, they fell upon Birney's unprotected right flank in the wheat field. Birney's men were completely unprepared for an attack from the rear, but even then they turned around and fired a volley at the Confederates. A moment later, the Confederates literally pounced on the Federals. As soon as this happened, the Union troops took a step back, and then lunged at the Confederates. All this ended in a fatal round of hand-to-hand fighting. It was so brutal that I had to turn my face away until it finally ended.

Hand-to-hand fighting is brutal process of killing each other with fists and bayonets. One man will stab another in the stomach, then he in turn is stabbed in the back, then that man is shot to death by an officer's pistol, and then someone shoots the officer, and then he is beaten to death by someone who jumps on him and pounds away at him. All this goes on until one side or the other decides that they've had enough and withdraws. After a while, I heard cheering and looked up to see the Confederates withdrawing.

With the Rebels in retreat, Sickles ordered some more men across his salient to help Birney. One of Warren's aides said that it was the 147th New York, under Van Horne Ellis. Just as they reached a formation of fallen boulders— Warren calls it the Devil's Den — the first men were cut down by Confederate volley. The men of the 147th New York rushed into position behind the boulders as yet more Rebels charged out of the woods from the south. At first the New Yorkers gave the worse end to the Rebels, but as more and more Confederates came out of the woods and entangled with the Yankees it seemed impossible for them to hold out.

Finally, the Confederates began to give ground, inch by inch, foot by foot. After about ten minutes, the 147th New York had regained all its lost ground. There was a cost for it, though, and its lines were proportionately thinner.

To make up for the 147th's failure to link up with Birney, those men at the end of the line fell back in order to join the 147th, but the Rebels didn't like this one bit. They charged out again, swarming into the gap between Birney and Ellis. Ellis's men quickly began pouring fire into the Rebels open flank, but Birney's men were caught on the move and quickly retreated. Seizing the advantage, the Confederates sent a small party of snipers to face Birney in the wheat field. They then turned their main force toward Ellis in the Devil's Den. The Rebs west of Devil's Den had been hard hit, but now more Confederates swarmed from the woods and attacked the east side of Devil's Den.

Now the 147th had to turn around and fire at this new threat. As soon as the New Yorkers had their backs turned, the Rebels west of Devil's Den split up. Half followed the snipers into the wheat field, while the other half attacked the rear of Devil's Den. And now, with Birney completely occupied, more Confederates charged down the road to hit the northern end of Sickles's line.

Within moments, the Confederates hit both the flanks and center of Humphreys's line, and sent them reeling backward. The courage of soldiers on both sides was amazing in this brief yet bloody struggle. For a Confederate, charging the enemy was more of a race than it was a dodging game, as it was for us. On the Union's part, tiny specks of blue, as their comrades fled, would stand in the way of entire lines of Confederates. The men would stand there, as Confederates swarmed all around them, swinging their rifles around like mad furies.

After a little while, a sheet of smoke hid our view of the battle. When the smoke finally subsided, it was clear which side had won: the Rebels. Birney's line was cracked and broken, with men fleeing to the rear. Humphreys's line had fallen back, too. However, Andrew Humphreys rode out in front of his men, and they rallied to form a pitch-patch line. In the

Devil's Den, no men from either side could be seen.

Warren was suspicious about the absence of any troops in the vicinity of Devil's Den. To make sure that there really were no troops, he ordered the one cannon that was up here to fire into the center of the area. At the spot that the cannonball landed, we saw for a moment several Confederate infantrymen dashing helter-skelter away from the bomb. Sure enough, there were Rebels in the Devil's Den.

Warren realized instantly that the Rebs had almost complete possession of the field and hurried off to find reinforcements. He certainly was quick about it, for it was a matter of moments before a brigade of infantry moved up here. Now soldiers are marching all over the place and artillery trains are rumbling by. Warren hasn't returned yet, probably looking for more troops.

It looks like the Rebs are going to attack pretty soon, so I'd better start getting back to my regiment.

Same Day. About Midnight
Ruins of a Destroyed Farmhouse

I guess that I made another wrong prediction, but this one may prove more fatal to myself than thinking Sickles's Corps would hold out. It's so dark that if I didn't have matches and candles in my haversack, I wouldn't be writing this.

It all started out when I was going down Little Round Top, heading in the direction of Cemetery Ridge. I was almost to the bottom when I ran into a small party of Confederates. We both froze for a moment, but I was the first to recover. I turned around and ran as fast as I could back up the slope. The Confederates started firing at me, but by that time I was too far away for them to hit me.

When I reached the top, I found that the Rebels were already attacking the summit of the Little Round Top. A thin line of Unions stood, firing at the massed Confederates thirty yards away.

An officer rode up and asked me what regiment I was from. When he heard that I was from the 14th Michigan, he cocked his head to the side and said, "Don't you belong over there?" gesturing toward Cemetery Ridge. I responded that I had been sent to find out what was going on over here, but that I was trapped. The officer thought for a moment and then said, "We need every man possible, and we'd consider it a favor if a feller like you would help us fight off these Rebs." I didn't need to be told twice. I found an empty spot in the line, cocked my rifle, fired, loaded, cocked my rifle again, and fired again.

A few moments later, more Rebels appeared. They fired one more volley at us, then surged forward. In a few moments, we were face to face with what seemed like twenty thousand Rebs. With rifle barrels literally touching, both sides would let volley after volley fly into the enemy lines. It was almost impossible for a bullet not to find its mark, but at times a rifle barrel could get so hot that it would explode and kill its own master.

It was the goriest, bloodiest fight that I have ever seen. One Reb put a red handkerchief around his head. The color made an inviting target, and almost immediately a bullet cracked open his skull.

After a while, though, numbers began to tell. Our lines were slowly growing thinner, while the Rebels came on stronger and stronger. Finally, Confederate bullets uncovered a large gap in our lines. The Rebs jumped up and surged through the gap. We realized that we could no longer hold out, and stumbled backward.

The Rebels made their first goal one of the two cannon that were at the summit. But now, just as it seemed impossible to hold, reinforcements arrived. It was a regiment under Paddy O'Rorke in Weed's Brigade. General O'Rorke rode up to the officer I had spoken to only a few minutes earlier. "Well, we're here, courtesy of a man called Gouverneur Kemble Warren," he said. "I guess we'll just go in and give 'em hell!"

With that, Paddy O'Rorke spurred his horse and rode out in front of his regiment. The Rebels fell backward, then braced themselves. General O'Rorke brandished his sword, ready to lead the charge. Just then, a bullet struck him full in the head, and he fell dead to the ground.

Still, the men moved forward, and within a few minutes they had dislodged the Rebel position. We rushed forward to their aid, and within a few moments there was an organized position ready to fire. It was at this moment that the Rebs chose to fire, though, and we were caught off our guard. At many points there were gaps. The Confederates were advancing forward, and we were definitely not ready for an assault.

Once again, at the very moment we needed it, reinforcements arrived. The other three regiments in Weed's Brigade had turned around and headed here when they learned that O'Rorke was already at the summit.

The Confederates had already lost their stomachs for fighting once O'Rorke arrived on the scene, and any more troops were simply too much for them. They retreated in a confused jumble, running this way and that.

I waited for half an hour to make sure that the Rebels were gone, then I headed for Cemetery Ridge. Once I reached the bottom of Little

Round Top, I turned west and began walking toward the ridge. After a moment I heard a noise. I moved over to a clump of bushes that provided adequate cover. Only two or three feet away was a party of Rebel skirmishers! If I know anything about attacking, then I know that large bodies of infantry follow close behind skirmishers.

I wheeled around just in time to see a company of Reb Infantry moving forward in rows of five, six ranks deep. Behind it were thousands of other companies, advancing forward in the same formation.

All of us were caught completely off our guards, but I regained my senses first, as what had happened the first time I ventured down Little Round Top. I dashed off, dodging the few bullets that were fired at me. I didn't stop running until I reached this farmhouse. It had been destroyed by a cannonball.

There was a tree next to the house, and I climbed it to see what was going on. When I reached the top, I was surprised and awed at the vast force of Confederates advancing toward the southern part of Cemetery Ridge. The 14th was too far west to be of any help. Apparently most of the II Corps had gone to help Sickles, leaving a huge gap in the line.

Only one regiment stood in the way of what looked like a whole division of Rebels. By its regimental flag, I could tell it was the 1st Minnesota Regiment. An average division has about five to six thousand men, while an average regiment has five hundred to a thousand men. What is more, the 1st Minnesota looked like an undersized regiment. There were only eight company flags. This meant that the 1st Minnesota had about 230 men.

Suddenly, with a shout, the 1st Minnesota lurched forward, charging downhill! The Rebs were surprised, and the Minnesota men got the first chance to fire. After a few minutes of reeling confusion, the 1st Minnesota used their advantage of catching the Rebs off guard, and divided them into three parts. A small group of Rebels stood on a low knoll holding the center. The 1st decided to pick this as their goal.

Rushing forward, they waited until they were

fifty yards away and then fired back at the Confederates. The Rebel flag went down, and most of the Confederates rushed to pick it up. At this moment, with several gaps in the Confederate lines, the 1st Minnesota charged ahead and destroyed most of the Reb position.

The Rebel left flank was still moving steadily forward with no one to block it, though! Suddenly, those Confederates who were climbing Cemetery Ridge stopped still in their tracks. From the other side of the ridge was heard a high pitched yelling sound. A moment later a Yankee regiment scrambled to the crest of the ridge just in time to pour a murderous fire down upon the Rebels waiting below.

In the scramble to get down the ridge, some of the Rebels ended up in the rear of the Minnesota men. Seizing this chance to at least inflict some damage on the enemy, the Rebs rallied and soon formed a wall around the regiment. In dismay, the 1st Minnesota desperately threw themselves against the sturdy wall of Confederates.

Finally, there was a small breakthrough.

Union men began pouring out of the circle toward the rear. I began counting, and I know that about forty-seven men got out before the Confederates closed the gap. Realizing that the situation was hopeless, many men began to surrender. A few fought desperately on, but most of them were slaughtered. After a little while, the Rebs had killed or captured all the men who hadn't escaped. Satisfied, they withdrew from their dangerous position and prepared to camp for the night.

Unfortunately, they didn't retreat far enough, and I'm trapped behind enemy lines. I don't really know how I can get through the Rebel camp without running into any pickets, but I guess that I'll have to try.

July 3. Noon
Cemetery Ridge

I made it back! It really wasn't very hard getting through the camp, but as I was going toward it from the farmhouse, I had no idea of how safe it would be.

I had only gone a couple of steps when I tripped. As I got up, I realized that I was still in my Union uniform. With all the campfires in the Rebel camp, the pickets and sentries would surely notice I was in it. I thought for a moment, tore a piece of paper out of this journal, then scribbled something on it.

I walked on. Fortunately for me, the Rebs were all inside their tents, all except the sentries. As I walked cautiously on, a picket stepped in front of me.

"Surrender!" he said. "You've got no hope of fighting it out."

Acting like this was all a big secret, I whispered to him: "I'm a spy. Here's my permit."

I handed him the piece of paper. As soon as his face was down, I thwacked him in the stomach with the butt of my rifle. He let out a low moan, but didn't scream. He wasn't dead, but he would stay unconscious long enough for me to escape.

As soon as I made it to the top of Cemetery Ridge, I was confronted by another problem: the *Union* pickets. I could tell from a long distance away that there were more of them than there had been Confederate pickets. When they saw me, they weren't much more polite than the Rebel had been. I said: "I'm with the 14th Michigan."

"How do we know you're not a spy?"

"Take me to the 14th, If nobody there knows me, you can do what you want with me."

"All right."

As soon as we got to the regiment, I went straight to the colonel's tent. Colonel Racker was still awake, studying some maps.

"Well, I'm back!"

"Aren't you a little late?"

I nodded, and gave him his pocket watch back. Just then one of the sentries burst in.

"Colonel, sir, Do you know this man?"

The Colonel gave him the strangest look, and then answered:

"Yes, I do. Of course I do. He's with my regiment!"

The sentry was more than embarrassed, and he stumbled out of the tent, and I went to my own tent. Johnny was already asleep, so he was quite surprised in the morning when he woke up and found me sleeping next to him. Apparently, everyone in the regiment thought I was dead!

It is scary to see the enemy massing for attack on the ridge across from us. It is going to be a massive one, and it appears that the enemy is going to attack the exact spot that we are at. We are positioned behind a low stone wall, and all morning we have been stacking rods and sticks on top of it to provide better cover.

Just south of where we are positioned, the stone wall juts forward at a place called the "Angle." Hancock, Meade, and some other officers are eating stew near the Angle. They are discussing plans also, and it seems like Meade agrees that the Rebs are going to attack right here, but refuses to bring more men to the ridge. Why he is doing this I do not know, but it's going to be quite hard to repulse any attack with the small handful of men stationed up here.

Same Day. 1:15 P.M.
Cemetery Ridge

I can hardly think what with the constant booming of shells above me! Not ten minutes ago, at precisely 1:07, several cannonballs were fired at us, blowing up two hay wagons. This salvo was followed by explosion after explosion, all aimed at us by hundreds of Rebel cannon on the ridge facing us. We all jumped flat on the ground for fear of being hit.

As far as I can see, none of the infantrymen have been killed, but the artillerymen manning the cannon just behind us have been hard hit. After a moment or two, our cannon opened up and fired back.

It is frightening to know that at any moment a cannonball may hit you on the back and kill you. I hope to God that we may repulse the on-coming attack.

July 4. 5:00 P.M.
Seminary Ridge

Due to the wound in my left arm, and the battle yesterday, I haven't been able to tell about what happened on July 3. I guess I'll begin where I left off last time.

At first we thought that the artillery bombardment was only a short, preliminary one, meant to weaken our defenses in preparation for the oncoming attack. It became apparent, though, after an hour of firing passed by, that the Rebel gunners meant to clear us off the ridge or run out of ammunition. It's a good thing that they fired too far, or else they might have succeeded.

The bombardment continued until 3:10 P.M. The Rebs had either run out of ammunition, or too many of their gunners had been killed. It was a good thing, too, for our gunners had mostly run out of ammunition and it was too dangerous to bring more to the guns without the wagons being blown up. A moment later, the assault began.

It was no ordinary attack, it was very majestic but very terrifying. The Rebs moved forward slowly, rifles shouldered, officers leading the way. There was a mysterious dignity about it, as if those making the attack meant to give their lives in order to win, or else give up the war.

It was unlike any normal charge, where men run as fast as they can, screaming, and moving quickly toward the enemy lines. This charge was slow, drummers and fifers playing their instruments, men walking. It was as if they were on dress parade, marching across the two-mile valley.

As they moved out, the momentary silence on our part that had followed the artillery bombardment was broken. We stood up, some whispering, others talking loudly.

"So they *are* making an infantry attack, after all."

"Here they come!"

"Just look at how foolish they are. When they get fifty yards away, they'll be the easiest targets I've ever seen."

"Come on, you Johnnies, come on."

They passed through the woods, then by houses and barns, and then through the fields of corn and wheat. Then our cannons, which had gotten more shells, opened fire. As one of the soldiers said, they were definitely easy targets. Wagon-wide swathes were cut open in the Confederate lines, but more men simply filled the gaps and moved forward.

Now a party of horsemen rode to the front of the line, one Rebel general leading them. The cannons, which were constantly firing, causing confusion and disorder among the Rebs, blocked our vision with smoke. When it finally thinned out, a bloody, riderless horse rode out in front of the men, then it rode back toward the Confederate lines.

The Rebels were only fifty yards away, now. They were blocked by a fence, and as they tried to climb over it, Colonel Racker gave the order to fire. The Confederates fell backward, then came forward again. They were running quickly, now that they were being fired on. Ten men would rush forward, only to fall down, never to get up again.

Now the cannon had accidentally blasted a hole in the fence, and the Rebs poured through. Another leader pushed his way to the front. This Confederate general was on foot. He had stuck his hat on the top of his sword, and was leading the charge.

Some of the Rebels stopped to fire, and left a large gap in the Angle. Cheering, the Rebs poured up onto the stone wall, killing all defending the Angle. In alarm, Colonel Racker ordered the 14th to abandon its position and attack the Confederates in the Angle. Just then a bullet hit him square in the neck, killing him instantly.

We all turned around to see yet more Rebels advancing to attack our position. In desperation and without a leader, most of the men rushed back to the original position. But the lieutenant ordered us to halt.

"Men, we have our orders. I don't command the other companies, but we are going to attack the Angle. CHARGE!"

We ran forward. The lieutenant, carrying the flag, was in the center. Johnny, his son, was next to him. I was on the other side of Johnny. The

Confederate general with his hat on his sword had just leaped over the stone wall, and was leading a party of men toward one of the guns. More Rebels poured over the stone wall and began firing at us. In the first volley, the lieutenant was hit by a bullet in the side. Johnny picked up the flag and ran forward. Another man pushed his way to the front of the line at the same time, Sergeant Emath. With Lieutenant Thompson down, Sergeant Emath was now in charge of the company.

Emath stopped a few paces from the cannon that the Reb general was now reaching somewhat possessively for. He fired once, hitting the man in the side. The Confederate leaped back up, grabbed the barrel of the cannon and struck out with his sword at the Sergeant. Emath leaped backward and fired again at the Rebel, this time hitting him in the stomach. The Reb general fell to the ground.

More and more Confederates were leaping over the wall and firing at us. Now Johnny went down with a bullet in his armpit. I turned around and asked Johnny if he were all right. His simple answer was: "You take the colors. I'll be fine."

A bit doubtful, I picked up the flag and moved forward. Just then, I heard a loud scream as more Union men poured into the Angle. Winfield Scott Hancock was leading them, but as he neared the cannon that Emath was still resting at after his debacle with the Rebel general, another Rebel volley swept down the front rank of men. With many others, Sergeant Emath and General Hancock went down.

But still the men Hancock had brought charged forward. It was obvious that the Confederates were outnumbered, and many of them stumbled back across the wall and retreated toward the ridge that I am standing on right now. (I heard that it is called Seminary Ridge.) A few fought stubbornly on, though, and as we moved forward I was shot in the left arm.

The company had been shot to pieces, and no one was able to pick the flag up. It didn't matter very much, though, for the Rebels had given up. In desperate retreat, they dashed back to Seminary Ridge, hoping that they would be lucky enough to make it.

While my left arm was wounded, I could still walk around. With the Rebs in full retreat, those in my company who could move around helped bring those who couldn't back to the regiment. The Confederate attack on the rest of the 14th was very undermanned, but it wasn't very easily repulsed. This was partly because of their determination, and partly because of our lack of leadership.

Of the original 29 men in Company D, 10 men are still alive, but only one is in good health and has not been shot at all. Not just the company, but the regiment has been decimated. Of the original 576 men, only 259 are still alive, 132 of which are not wounded.

There is better news also. I am *extremely* relieved that Lieutenant Thompson, Johnny Thompson, Sergeant Emath, and Corporal Unda are alive, though badly wounded. As for myself, my arm is in much better condition.

On Colonel Racker's death, Major Bellport

took command of the regiment, on account of his bravery, Sergeant Emath has gotten a minor promotion. He is now Command Sergeant Major Emath. Command Sergeant Major means almost nothing in military standards, except for one difference: more pay. Even still, he is very proud.

By 3:00 P.M. today, one day after the charge, Company D is to be dissolved. I am now in Company A. Company A's commander, Lieutenant Grizzard, was killed, and so when Lieutenant Thompson recovers, he will command Company A.

By 3:00 the entire Rebel army had withdrawn. One hour later, with thousands of men cheering, we marched through crowds of cheering civilians in Gettysburg and moved on to Seminary Ridge.

I will never forget some of these moments that I have seen; the way the Rebels moved forward yesterday, how daring and dedicated they were. But neither will I forget how equally well some of our men fought back. After this victory, I've made a decision: after all, I *am* going to reenlist!

Characters: Historical and Fictional

In *The Diary of Edward Daniel Phillips*, it may be confusing to tell which characters are real and which were made up. To avoid any confusion, here is a list of which are and which aren't.

Historical Characters	Fictional Characters*
George Meade	Edward Daniel Phillips
Winfield Scott Hancock	Johnny Thompson
Robert E. Lee	Lieutenant Thompson
John Reynolds	John Phillips**
John Buford	Karl Malz
Joseph Hooker	Colonel Racker
Abner Doubleday	Sergeant Rice
Henry Heth	Sergeant Emath
Daniel Sickles	Corporal Unda
Gouverneur Kemble Warren	Captain Abraham
David Birney	
Andrew Humphreys	* All of the characters in the 14th Michigan are made up.
Van Horne Ellis	
Paddy O'Rorke	** Edward's older brother, at this time fighting in Grant's Army of the Tennessee
General Weed	
Ulysses Grant	

About the Author

———❖———

Of writing *The Diary of Edward Daniel Phillips,* Nathan Sadasivan says, "I first heard about the Scholastic contest at a library program. I got very excited and started working on it immediately. About one quarter of the way through, my enthusiasm died down. I started running out of ideas, and I got bored with writing it out. I started doing it less and less. Eventually, I squeezed through that phase and got to more exciting parts. By mid-November, I was done. Next came the proofreading. It took almost as long to correct the journal as it did to write it. In the end, we mailed it only two or three days before the deadline!

"Near the beginning of third grade, we set off on a vacation around the eastern half of America. We turned north along the Atlantic coast, from Georgia to Maryland (which is dotted with Civil War battlefields). We visited several Civil War sites, including Fort Sumter, where the war began, and Appomattox, where the war ended. Although I was a little reluctant to go to any of them, I came back from the trip a Civil War buff."

Nathan is eleven years old. He has two brothers, who are eight and nine, and one sister, who is three years old. This contest was the first writing contest he entered. Since then, he's entered six more. Nathan lives in Brighton, Michigan.

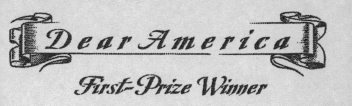

Dear America
First-Prize Winner

VOLCANO OF MONT PELÉE

THE DIARY OF NICOLE MAILHOT
SAINT PIERRE, MARTINIQUE, CARIBBEAN, 1902

BY NICOLE HILLYARD

SAINT-PIERRE, MARTINIQUE, CARIBBEAN, 1902

APRIL 15, 1902

Dear Diary,

What a beautiful day it was here in Saint-Pierre, Martinique, "The Paris of the Caribbean." My mère (mother), my brothers Jean-Luc, Pelée, and I just go back from an exciting and fun day.

We got up early and walked to Mr. Léon Compère-Léandre's, the shoemaker's house. He just got finished fixing an old pair of shoes for my little brother Pelée. Pelée just turned one last month and is starting to run quite fast now. My mère and père (father) say Pelée is a very healthy and strong-willed little boy. That is why they named him after our 4,430-foot volcano, Mont Pelée. Mont Pelée is on the northern end of our tropical island. Mère and Père said that Mont Pelée can be strong-willed, too. Once, a long time ago, it erupted in 1727. Mont Pelée is quiet now, but not my brother Pelée. I think they named him Pelée because he's loud and erupts like a volcano in his pants.

On our way to Mr. Compère-Léandre, we stopped at my best friend Monique Léger's house. We have so much fun together. Many people say we look like sisters. We both are the same height. We have brown hair and eyes and we're both nine years old. I say we are more like twins. We pretend that sometimes.

Mrs. Léger and Mère were talking about the supplies we will need for our trip to America. My père has been saying for the last year that we are moving to Rhode Island in America as soon as he finishes building our boat. Mr. Léger and my pére are the best ship makers in the world and they need good shipbuilders in America. They will pay our families good money over there. Père told Mère today that the boat is almost finished. My best friend, Monique, and her family will be coming, too. Monique and I really don't want to go to America. It is so beautiful here in Saint-Pierre. Rhode Island seems so far away and strange. Père says the trip will only take five to seven days, depending on the winds. I'm glad Monique and I have each other and two more months left here, before we go.

After our stop at the shoemaker's, Monique and Mrs. Léger came into town with us. We picked up lots of supplies like salt, flour, grains, and sugar for the trip. My older brother, Jean-Luc, saw a paper hanging on the window of the store. It said there is a twenty-five-year-old prisoner, Auguste Ciparis, being held in the Cité's dungeon for murder. The paper said he is going to be hung on May 8. Jean-Luc asked if we could go see him. I started to shake. Just the thought of it scared me. Mère said, "No, there is no point in seeing him, he is a bad man." I was happy she said that. I asked Mère, "What if he were to escape before May 8. Jean-Luc said that then he would come after Monique and me." Mère scolded him. Then she assured us that it could never happen because the dungeon is a small, dark room with thick, heavy walls. It would be impossible to escape. Jean-Luc thinks he's so tough but I think he's foolish even though he is three years older than I am.

In front of the chocolate shop, there was a group of townspeople. They were clanging all kinds of instruments. I saw flutes, saxophones, tubas, and drums. The drums were the loudest. They hurt my ears. I asked Mère what they were doing. She told me that they were practicing for the parade the town was going to have soon. Mr. Louis Mouttet is the governor of Martinique and the election is coming up soon. The parade was for the upcoming election. I can't wait to see it. It looked like it would be a lot of fun.

We all stopped at the shipyard on our way home. We wanted to see how Père was doing on the boat. Père was right he was almost finished. It was a big boat. It had a cooking room and four bedrooms downstairs. Two rooms are for our family and two are for Monique's family. There were lots of places to store things, too. Mère put some of the supplies away. She said there was no sense taking them to the house, just to bring them back again. It looked like Père had already picked up many supplies too. Pelée wanted to play with all the new supplies. In fact, he was making quite a mess. Mère wasn't too happy.

Mère told us to go out and play on the beach with Pelée for a while. She wanted to straighten things up and talk to Père alone. We didn't mind because we love the beach.

The beach is the most beautiful place in the whole world. Monique and I can play there all day, every day. There is so much to do there, we never get bored. Sometimes we play house, or store. Other times we pretend we are princesses in a castle. But today we decided to chase after Pelée and bury him in the sand up to his waist. He likes that. When he would get free, we would pretend to close our eyes and count to five. That way he would have a head start on us. Then we would chase him again.

After playing on the beach we went home. Jean-Luc and I showed Mère a shortcut through the woods. We were all very tired. Pelée fell asleep on Mère's shoulder. Mère said she thinks he will sleep the whole night tonight. I know I will. It's 9:00 P.M. and Mère told me to shut off the lantern and go to sleep now. So I will write again soon.

— Nicole

APRIL 27, 1902

Dear Diary,

Sorry I haven't written in the past twelve days. We have been very busy packing the boat for America. Père says we are going sooner than expected. It looks like the volcano is becoming active again. It has been scary. On April 23, the earth began to shake and we heard three loud explosions. They seemed to be inside the mountain. Some of our plates and bowls fell off the shelves and broke. Monique said that their wall in the bedroom has a big crack in it now.

On the twenty-fifth, the volcano started to spit ash and gas. It has been covering everything and everyone with gray dust. People are having a hard time breathing because of the gases. My throat has been sore and my eyes feel like they are burning all the time. Père says that a lot of animals in Saint-Pierre have been dying because of the poisonous gases. They suffocated. Sometimes I feel like I am suffocating, too. Mère and Père have made us stay inside the house and keep the doors and windows closed except when we go to school. Whenever we leave the house, we cover our mouths with a piece of cloth.

On April 27, some volcano experts went up the side of the volcano. They found that the small crater that has been dry since 1851 is now a lake filled with water. Père says that this is not a good sign. Both my parents and Monique's parents have decided to leave the island as soon as we can.

— Nicole

MAY 2, 1902

Dear Diary,

At 11:30 A.M. today, an explosion happened on Mont Pelée. We were all at school doing math. Everybody jumped out of their seats and ran to the window. We saw a giant cloud of steam coming out of the volcano. It was also spitting rocks and more ash out, too. A few minutes later tremendous bolts of lightning flashed up from the small crater that Père had talked about earlier. Most of the boys in my class thought it was an awesome sight. The rest of the class remained quiet. Our teacher, Mrs. Boisvert, looked scared but tried not to show it. That made me scared. I didn't tell anyone that I was scared, because I didn't want them to think I was acting like a baby. Mrs. Boisvert thought it was best if we all went home for the day. She told us to go straight home and not to go anywhere else. Monique, Jean-Luc, and I liked that idea, too. So we grabbed our books, ran out the door, and started home.

When we got outside, it looked like it was snowing out. Soft pieces of gray ash were falling all around us. It was covering everything. Monique and I were having fun making footprints and designs in it as we walked. On our way home, we noticed that all the stores were closing down for the day, too. Then it began to rain very hard. I have never seen anything like it. It was black rain. This was probably because of all the ash. So we ran the rest of the way home.

When Mère saw us, she laughed and said that Jean-Luc and I looked like two black cats that almost drowned. She told us to take a bath and scrub the soot off. That is exactly what we had to do: scrub, scrub, and scrub. It took a lot of scrubbing. It just didn't want to come off. Mère helped me scrub. My skin was turning red and began to hurt from all the scrubbing. Finally, she said that was enough scrubbing and that I looked clean enough. Jean-Luc took his bath next and Mère told him to scrub really well. Every time he came out Mère told him to go bathe again and scrub a little harder. She offered to help him, but he didn't want her in there while he was naked. He thinks he is all grown up. Mère made him go in the bath five times. Jean-Luc wasn't very happy but I thought it was funny.

When Père came home, he said that the entire northern half of the island of Martinique disappeared under a coating of ash today. And he said the town looked like a ghost town. Everything in Saint-Pierre came to a halt. The few who ventured out move silently through the deserted streets and their footsteps were muffled by the thick layer of dust and ash.

We told Père all about the black rain and how hard it was to get off. He explained that this could happen when ash particles and moisture mixed together and, as a result, it causes torrential rainfall. It has been raining ever since. Père told us it was bedtime and he wanted to talk to Mère now. I couldn't sleep after all that has happened today. I overheard Père talking to Mère in the kitchen. Père was told by some volcano experts that the level of the water in the Crater Lake was getting higher and higher because of all the rain. The temperature of the water was also rising, so high that the water was starting to boil in the crater. They feel that the volcano may erupt soon. He sounded nervous and said we have to leave the island this week. Mère said everyone in town is talking of leaving, too. But the governor of Martinique, Louis Mouttet, is assuring everybody it is safe to stay. Mr. Mouttet said he has seen this happen before and the volcano is not going to erupt. He said that even if the volcano erupted, they had nothing to worry about. Saint-Pierre is located at the foot of Mont Pelée and because of the shape of the mountain, lava would not flow into Saint-Pierre. For this reason people from the countryside were actually coming into the city for safety. He is even moving his family to Saint-Pierre this week to prove how safe it is. Père yelled angrily that he's no expert; he is a fool. Père never did like Mr. Mouttet.

I'm starting not to mind the idea of leaving anymore. The thought of a volcano erupting scares me more than going to Rhode Island. I don't think I feel safe here anymore.

— Nicole

MAY 8, 1902
EVENING

Dear Diary,

A lot has happened in the last six days. Our life is not the same as it was a few days ago. On May 5, Père and Mr. Léger decided it was time we left the island. At about 12:30 P.M. We gathered the rest of our things and began to leave for the boat. Then, suddenly, we heard a thunderous roar. The side of the Crater Lake gave way. The hot water with volcanic ash formed a thin mud and began to slide down a side of the mountain nearby. It destroyed everything in its path. Père said that it was about a half-mile wide and traveled about one mile per minute. At 12:33 P.M., the avalanche of mud reached the sea, three miles from the volcano. The sugar mill that we were just at, not too long ago, was gone. It took only an instant and the boiling mud spread over the entire mill and killed everyone inside. Père said that forty people worked inside. The only thing that was left was the factory's tall smokestacks. Farmers and villagers from other districts rushed to Saint-Pierre for protection, while others in Saint-Pierre were trying to leave, like us. There was a lot of confusion. On our way to the boat, soldiers posted along the roads stopped us. They told us all to go home. No one was allowed to leave. The reason? Louis Mouttet, the governor of Martinique, wanted to make sure that the people remain in the city to vote for him in the upcoming election!

Père and Mr. Léger were mad. Mr. Léger said no one was going to stop him and began to push through the soldiers. They arrested him and put him in a house nearby. We went back to our home and Monique and Mrs. Léger came with us. Père told us to go down to the boat tonight, after midnight and stay there. He wanted us to take the shortcut that we showed Mère earlier. We could only take what we could carry. He said for us not to let anyone see us or know that we are there. He was going to try to free Mr. Léger.

He said if he wasn't back in two days, for us to leave him behind. We didn't like that idea at all.

That night we made it to the boat safely and no one knew. We waited patiently for Père and Mr. Léger.

Our wait seemed like forever. We didn't know what was happening to Mr. Léger or Père. I kept thinking, *"What if they arrested Père, too. We wouldn't leave without him, would we?"* We waited and waited for two days and two nights. We were suppose to leave but Mère and Mrs. Léger couldn't. Mère said we would wait till daybreak and see if they came then.

At about 6:30 A.M. this morning Mère and Mrs. Léger started preparing the boat for leaving. At 7:00 A.M. we saw Mr. Léger and Père coming slowly across the sand. They looked like they were hurt. We hurried them to the boat. When Mère asked what happened to them, Père told us that he tried to talk to the soldiers about freeing Mr. Léger. They laughed and grabbed him and beat him up. They then threw him in with Mr. Léger, who was beat up, too. The soldiers knew that they could barely move so they didn't watch them very well. Père and Mr. Léger looked for their first chance to get away. They tried as fast as they could to get to the boat sooner but they weren't able. I'm so glad we waited and they were, too.

We began to set sail. It was a bright, clear morning. We could hear the church bells chiming. At 7:52 A.M., when we were about a half a mile away, Monique began to yell good-bye to the island. We all looked back at the island and we saw the tall column of steam and ash rising above Mont Pelée. We were all used to that sight by now. Jean-Luc, Pelée, and I all joined in with Monique in saying good-bye. At 7:59 A.M., all at once, four loud bangs came out from the volcano. It sounded like a thousand cannons, all going off at the same time. The side of the mountain exploded and a huge, glowing cloud of superhot steam, molten lava, and giant boulders burst out of the crater. They were aimed directly at Saint-Pierre. Mère and Père told us not to look and to go downstairs in the boat. We couldn't believe our eyes. All was quiet. I don't feel much like writing anymore today. I will write again soon.

— Nicole

May 17, 1902

Dear Diary,

We arrived in Rhode Island two days ago and it isn't so bad here. We are still living on the boat for now until Père and Mr. Léger find a place for us to live. People are all talking about the volcanic explosion that happened in Saint-Pierre. The newspaper had a big article on it. The explosion was called a nuée ardente explosion. The paper said the boulders that we saw shoot from the crater were traveling about three hundred miles per hour. The red glowing cloud made a hurricane force and leveled everything in its path. The surge of steam was believed to be about 1,800 degrees Fahrenheit. It melted glass, twisted the heaviest steel beams, and turned wood into charcoal instantly. Everyone who tried to breathe the air died immediately. The heat completely shriveled their lungs. While the cloud hung over the city, there were no fires, since there is not enough oxygen to feed the flames. But as soon as the cloud was gone, the air rushed in and fires burst out all over, burning to a crisp everything that was left. By 8:02 A.M. it was all over. It makes me sad to think that in three minutes 34,000 people were killed by the volcano.

Besides us, only two people survived the disaster. One was the shoemaker, Léon Compère-Léandre, whose house somehow escaped the eruption. He told the experts, "I was seated on the doorstep of my house, and all of a sudden, I felt a terrible wind blowing, the earth began to tremble and the sky grew dark. I turned to go into the house . . . and felt my arms and legs burning, also my body. Crazed and almost overcome, I threw myself upon a bed, inert and awaiting death. My senses returned to me in about an hour, when I beheld the roof burning." He was badly burned but somehow he got to the next village, where he got help. No one can guess how Mr. Compère-Léandre managed to live through the volcano while everyone else died from the heat and flames.

The other man to escape was the murderer Auguste Ciparis. He was going to be hung that day. He had no idea of what was happening until he felt a blast of heat force its way through the small opening of the grated window, over the door. His back and legs were badly burned but it didn't kill him. Mr. Ciparis was stuck in the cell for four days in pain, with no food or water. Finally, a rescue team from the neighboring town freed him. He is going to have permanent scars but he is alive. Because of everything he went through, the authorities decided to pardon him for his crime. Mr. Ciparis said he thinks he will work for a circus and call his act "The Prisoner of Saint-Pierre." That is one circus I don't want to see.

I'm glad we moved to America. But I will never forget my beloved home in Saint-Pierre. — Nicole

About the Author

Of writing *Volcano of Mont Pelée,* Nicole Hillyard says, "I like excitement and action. I was originally going to base my story on a Hawaiian volcano but in my research I came across the volcano of Mont Pelée. As I read on, I learned of the tragedy that happened there. I did more research and borrowed three more books from my library; I also used some encyclopedias we had at home. I had to do extra research to make sure my story was historically accurate.

"In my story, the main character, her family, and friends are fictional but the shoemaker and the prisoner are real; they were the only two people to survive the volcano. The governor was also real; he posted guards so no one could leave the island or town. He moved his family to Saint-Pierre to prove to people how safe it was, and later perished along with his family and 34,000 others the day the volcano erupted.

"I tried to pretend in my mind that I was the Nicole in the story. I kept asking myself how I would feel if these things happened to me. I wrote these feelings down as best I could. During the two months it took me to write the diary, I had to keep going back to my research to make sure the details were accurate. My advice to other children is to work hard and keep reading and writing."

Nicole Ashley Hillyard is nine years old and lives in Londonderry, New Hampshire. She is home-schooled, and her hobbies are gymnastics, ballet, art, writing, and crafts. She also plays the flute and collects cars. Grand-prize winner Jodie Hillyard is Nicole's sister.